Officers and Educators

MERGING OUR WORLDS

Deputy John Calvert and Dr. Heather Calvert

Principal Principles Publications

United States of America

Authors/Deputy John Calvert, Dr. Heather Calvert.

info@calvertenterprises.com

https://www.calvertenterprises.com

Ordering Information:

Quantity sales. Special discounts are available on quantity purchases by corporations, associations, and others. For details, contact the "Special Sales Department" at the address above.

Officers and Educators: Merging Our Worlds/ Calvert —1st ed.

ISBN Paperback 979-8-9918416-6-5

Cover Image Credit: Lftikhar Alam Creative Market

Contents

Table of Contents

"School safety isn't a one-person job; it is everyone's job. When we realize we are all on the same team, fighting the common problem, we can make great strides in the climate and culture of our schools."

- John and Heather

Dedication and Acknowledgements

This book is dedicated to a variety of people who have helped drive the passion that we both have for this topic. First, to our own children, Abigail and John, you are each the greatest gifts we could receive from God. Thank you for listening to our dinner table conversations, sharing your thoughts and beliefs, and for being the amazing humans you are. To our family members, who have watched and listened as we always pushed for more with our professional careers, thank you. You are as much a part of making this work come to life as anyone. Thank you to Janet, Chuck, Randy, Joyce, and Sandy for watching the kids and helping to get them to and from all the places they needed to be while we presented this work across the nation.

Second, to all of our professional colleagues, we thank you for shaping our beliefs and walking this road with us. Each of you, no matter how many years ago we worked together, have been a part of this journey. You were with us as we navigated these situations in real time. Heather would like to give a special shout-out to Officer Kelly Roberts for being one of the first officers she interacted with as an administrator. Officer Roberts, thank you for always being kind, compassionate, and striving every day to make our schools safe places for students and staff. You never hesitated to spend the time to talk with me to make sure I understood your world, you asked me questions about mine, and you proved to me that we can merge our worlds if we keep trying. John would like to give a special shout-out to John Rundle, my very first Superintendent as a school resource officer (SRO). Mr. Rundle, thank you for taking a chance on me and showing me how I could fit in and make a positive difference in the climate and culture in school buildings. Thank you for accepting my big goofy personality—and pushing back when you felt it best. Most importantly, thank you for always having a smile on your face and for never wavering in your trust in me to make the best decisions to keep our schools safe. It is always a GREAT day to be a Panther!

Third, to everyone who has sat in one of our sessions and to the organizations who have trusted us with breakout and keynote sessions, we thank you for believing in our message. We hope to make you proud by continuing this work, and we hope that you are still fighting to merge these worlds.

Finally, and most importantly, we thank God for bringing us together, putting us in the professional roles that we have, and allowing us to live our passions every day. Without Him, we would not be where we are today. Jeremiah 29:11.

Pull Up a Chair

We would like to welcome you to our dinner table. Like many families, we try to prioritize eating at the table every evening. We started this nightly tradition when we got married, sharing stories of a teacher and law enforcement officer both young in our careers. At the time, these worlds were not even in the same universe for us. We listened to each other, empathized, offered advice, and moved on to the next day. As a point of reference, at this time, our nation was post-Columbine but pre-Sandy Hook. In this era of our lives, school safety was not a popular topic, and as a country, it was not a focus.

Over the next five years, we added two children to our dinner table and two dogs eagerly waiting next to the table for "shared" food. We also each began advancing in our careers. By the time our daughter was five and our son was two, John had transitioned into the role of a School Resource Officer (SRO). Heather had completed her Master's Degree in Curriculum and Instruction and was working on her Doctorate in Educational Leadership. She had transitioned out of the classroom, spent two years as an Instructional Coach, and moved into the world of school administration. Sadly, school violence had seen a dramatic increase, and as a country, we suffered many tragedies. School safety had become a hot topic and something that school districts and communities were all working through in different ways. At this point, the conversations around our table shifted dramatically. As our daughter entered kindergarten, we now experienced school safety from not only two different professional worlds, but also as parents. These three lenses clashed almost daily, and we often struggled through conversations.

One revelation we both had during these early conversations was our experiences in school, which was well before school safety became a focal point. We remember propped-open recess doors, parents able to help with parties and bring us lunch without stopping by the office, and never a concern that something would happen at the Friday night football or basketball game. This is important to consider. As students, John only participated in one lockdown drill in his K-12 career during 6th grade, while Heather was never involved in a lockdown drill as a student. Yet here we were, as leaders in our school districts, and we were supposed to provide guidance to staff and students on multiple aspects of school safety.

Fast forward to our current reality, and our daughter is now finishing her eighth-grade year and ready to enter high school. Our son is finishing his fifth-grade year and ready to enter middle school. Heather is still a school administrator and has worked in three school districts. After 6 years as a School Resource Officer, John transitioned to a bigger role at the Kansas State Department of Education supporting school safety in all public school districts in Kansas. Our dinner table conversations now include our children as active participants. We like to go around our table and each share our "peak" and "pit" of the day (high and low points). Oftentimes, our conversations have nothing to do with school or school safety. Sometimes, school safety conversations arise from something that we share. But sometimes, it comes from things one of our kids shares. As adults, we tend to forget to include an important voice in our schools: the students. Those conversations throughout the years have allowed us to understand school safety from a student perspective as well. Now, we understand that the view of two students does not represent the view of every student. However, their perspective and experiences often tell us things we had not previously considered. Our own kids don't know a world without doing lockdown drills. To them it is normal, so it is important to gauge their feelings and thoughts on what is going on in their school.

What became a normal topic of conversation around our dinner table transformed over time into a passion project for us. As the years have passed, we have seen firsthand an increase in violent events on school campuses nationwide, and we have watched school safety become politicized in many ways. In this work, we stay out of the political arena because it polarizes and creates sides. School safety has no sides, and we can't afford for anyone to lose. We believe we must stop fighting each other and merge our worlds to fight the problems together. While it is clear to see where this work fits in for law enforcement, it is also the utmost goal of any educator. In education, our mission will always be to provide students with high-quality learning experiences, but we can never hope to accomplish that if our schools aren't safe. As we worked through issues each day, we began to see ways in which we could merge our worlds and create safer spaces for our students. The question then became, how do we tackle this and share these breakthrough moments we had at our table with others?

As we began pondering how to share this work, we realized that even in today's world there is very little, if anything at all, that is being done in our separate worlds, as educators and law enforcement officers, to help knock down the barriers and get us out of our silos to merge our worlds. Again, this is no one's fault, and it is not about pointing fingers. We looked back on our biggest struggles and found that there are five major struggles hat must be worked through to merge our worlds. We developed a one-hour presentation covering all five of these topics and began presenting at local conferences. We then had a school district ask us to transform this work into a four-hour workshop with the middle and high school administrators and the school district police department. From there, this presentation has continued to grow. It has been presented in a multitude of formats across the nation to various audiences, but the feedback has always been the same. Participants find value in the five merges and leave not only with applicable things they can easily implement but a new frame of mind when working with the other world.

We recognize that we are not the only two people struggling through difficult conversations about school safety, nor are we the only school administrator and law enforcement officer trying to figure out how to maintain a productive professional relationship. However, being married, there is no option to throw our hands up, quit, or "agree to disagree" with these emotionally charged issues. Our dinner table is where conversations were had, and lessons were learned in real-time. What started as a husband and wife venting about the events of the day and asking questions that had no answers has transformed into us recognizing that our shared experiences and lessons learned can benefit others in our respective roles who may be struggling with similar issues. As we learned from each other, we began to recognize the significant gap that often exists between the worlds of educators and law enforcement officers. This was the first major hurdle we had to acknowledge and address. When we dove into the possible reasons why, we realized that in all of our course work, professional development, and professional reading, not once was school safety or the successfully development of a collaborative relationship between educators and officers addressed. To put it another way, John had been a full-time law enforcement officer for six years and had hundreds of hours of training over that time. Yet, when he entered a school district for the first time, he had zero training on what school-based law enforcement could or should look like. Heather has a Bachelor's Degree in Education, a Master's Degree and Curriculum and Instruction, and a Doctorate in Educational Leadership, but not one minute of one class was devoted to school safety or interacting with law enforcement in any way. For those in either of these fields reading this, you are already nodding your head in agreement. For those not in these fields, it seems odd that roles as important as these would not be discussed and that there is such little work being done in the field to merge these worlds. There is a multitude of work being done to address school safety, but these are mainly guidelines, programs, or training on how to prepare structurally or during a school crisis. And that work is valid, needed, and well-received by both officers and educators. What is missing is the vast amount of work that can be accomplished for free by merging these worlds through adjusting our interactions.

You might be thinking, "Okay, but you don't know how it works in my district/town/city/school," and you are right. One thing that we realized through our professional roles is that school safety is addressed differently in each state, city, town, and school district. To be honest that is probably one reason why there is not much being done in the field to support those who are doing the work. There are more factors than we could begin to address if we chose to go down that rabbit hole. In all of our presentations, workshops, keynotes, etc., we have never found one school, district, or department that has the exact same set up for school safety. Some districts have their own police departments, some work with local law enforcement to have officers assigned to the schools, and some are only called when needed. For these reasons, we have chosen to address educators and officers in our work not using specific titles or position names. We believe that no matter what position you find yourself working in, you can see where you fit into these merges. By working together and having brutal, open, and honest conversations, we have developed five key merges for any educator and officer to better serve students, staff, and families. This work is never one-sided, and this book is meant to start the conversations between whoever is around your "dinner table."

How To Read This Book:

This book was written in such a way that you can read it alone, as a book study, or in a workshop format. In each chapter, you will find three distinct sections. The "The View from the Officer's World" sections are written by John, while "The View from the Educator's World" sections are written by Heather. Both our voices come together in "The Merge" sections. You might notice variances in the writing style and voices found in each section, and those were left intentionally.

If you are reading this book by yourself, we have included prompts to push your reflection and thinking at the end of each chapter. We urge you to reflect on your own professional practice and the interactions that you have. Please know that we believe you can still improve the relationship with the other world by engaging with a better insight as to what they are bringing to the table. If nothing else, you might alleviate some of your own frustrations.

We have found this work is best accomplished when both sides work through it together as either a book study or workshop model. At the end of each chapter, there are discussion questions that are meant to be discussed with each other. If you read this book as a book study, the conversation between the two worlds can use these questions as a starting point. If you are reading this in a workshop format, we recommend having teams that will work together, sit together. We then urge each participant to read the chapter introduction followed by "The View" section from the lens that best describes their profession. After each section is read, pause and reflect on your own practice. Then, read "The View" from the opposing world as you. At this point, we would recommend using a structure to guide the conversation about key takeaways each member has. Finally, read "The Merge" section and process through the discussion questions. In addition, at the end of the book, you will find scenarios that are meant to help teams work through 'real' situations.

No matter how you read this book, we would love to hear from you as you work through each merge.

CHAPTER 1

Speaking the Same Language

This chapter would have been really easy to write if we wanted to be basic. What is the first step and key to any successful relationship? Effective communication. We could have easily stopped there, and regurgitated ideas other authors have already stated regarding how adults can build stronger professional relationships by ensuring effective communication is happening. *We all get it.* Instead, we knew we had to dig deeper. **Why is it SO hard for educators and law enforcement officers to effectively communicate with each other?** Sure, we don't always spend a lot of time together in the same space, but that's not unique to just this professional relationship. Educators— most of us have itinerant staff who work in multiple buildings—and yet, we don't struggle to communicate at the depth that we do with officers. Law enforcement officers, there are many who work in the department that you never encounter, or you may be at a scene with different agencies and/or officers you've never even met. However, you can work with them and communicate perfectly fine. Right?

After many conversations around our dinner table, we realized there are two main reasons that we struggle to communicate with each other in a professional manner. The first is that we simply are not speaking the same language, verbally and nonverbally. The second is that we have very different views of communication while working in our respective fields that must be acknowledged. Again, while it may seem that this should be the easiest merge to make, it is actually the most difficult to work through, but it sets the groundwork for any future merges to be made.

As we said in the introduction, this work is most powerful when both sides commit to work through it together. However, if you find yourself in this work by yourself, don't fret. Not only do we hope to help you understand the other side's form of communication, we also hope to help you shift your thinking about the way you communicate. Little shifts can make a big difference, especially over time. We will say this often, but there is no right or wrong in this work. Both officers and educators are working hard to keep all of our schools safe, and keeping that at the forefront of the difficult work is imperative.

> *Both officers and educators are working hard to keep all of our schools safe, and keeping that at the forefront of the difficult work is imperative.*

The View from the Officer's World:

"Dispatch, show me 10-15 with a Code 1, 10-32, en route to signal 90. Copy starting when you're ready."

Most officers totally understand what that statement means, and we have probably all said something similar a hundred times. The interesting thing is that different jurisdictions across the country use different codes or signals, so there are some in law enforcement who are just as lost as the educators who are reading this! Some agencies now use "plain speech" when talking on the radio, except for a few codes/signals that represent potentially dangerous situations if people understand what we were talking about.

Officers don't just rely on our verbal communication when working in the field. I worked with a partner who knew what I was thinking or getting ready to do simply by looking at him. There were times where I would look at him and cross my arms and he would nod. What I was saying was, "I'm thinking we have enough to arrest," or "I think we should put this person in handcuffs." By nodding, he agreed.

One time my partner looked at me, and I could tell he was ready to arrest a suspect. I simply said, *"Stand by."* There was no need for further conversation. He understood that I needed more information before I felt comfortable moving forward. This type of communication saved time, and probably saved me from injury in some situations. It is important to note that being able to communicate nonverbally didn't happen overnight. It took time, many conversations, and trust between us to be able to communicate in these ways. When I would respond to an event in the school, I sometimes became frustrated that the other adults around me didn't understand what I was thinking or why it was important to do things my way.. Just like when I worked the streets, the relationship with other officers didn't come right away. I realized that the longer I was in the school, the stronger my relationship with administrators became to the point where we knew what the other was thinking.

When I was a school resource officer, I was a deputy for a county Sheriff's Office. I was responsible for three different school districts spanning over 20 minutes from one district to the other. Because of this, there were times where I would be the second or third responding officer to an incident that occurred inside one of "**my schools.**" When I first started, there was an incident where another officer responded while I was driving non-emergent to the school to assist. When I arrived, I found the officer and principal talking about the incident in the principal's office. The student was sitting in the main office, away from everyone else. I stepped in, not even shutting the door behind me, looked right at the officer, and said, *"Are we going 15 (10-15, arrest)? Do you need me to go signal 90 (transport to jail)?"* The officer knew exactly what I was saying. We had a conversation about the student, and the consequences right in front of the principal. When I was caught up, the principal looked at me, and said, *"Ok, what is going on? What did you guys say?"* Without even thinking about it, I had alienated the principal in his own office ... in his school! When I laughed and explained that I was asking the other officer if we were going to arrest the student, the principal's eyes got big and he said, *"Oh gosh, no!"* And in a matter of one sentence, everything was cleared up.

There would be a school consequence, but the principal also wanted an informational report taken to document the incident. Without realizing it, I had been speaking the language of law enforcement. However, I needed to recognize that there was another important voice who needed to be heard in the conversation. I always remembered that incident and tried to act as a translator in future conversations with officers when we were around educators. Officers, when we step into a school, it is important to realize that we are no longer on the streets. Our words mean something different, and most educators will not understand any codes that we use.

On the other side, there have been many conversations I have had with educators in which they would use words or phrases that I had never heard before or didn't quite understand. I would act like I completely understood because I didn't want anyone to think I was 'out of my depth.' After the meeting or conversation had ended, I would then text my wife asking for meaning and clarification. One time, during a meeting with the high school principal, he stated that he was suspending a student and would have to go to a manifestation hearing, but for this incident, it was worth it. I had no idea what a manifestation hearing was or why it would be used for this incident. When I got home, I tried to ask Heather what was going on, but I couldn't remember the term "manifestation hearing." I'm sure it took me several words and probably 10 minutes for her to figure out what I was trying to say. She provided me with the backstory as to what a manifestation hearing is and why some students and incidents must go to a hearing. This sparked even more questions from me, and we started going down the rabbit hole. "What is an IEP? What does this mean for schools? What does this mean for law enforcement?" She then posed the question to me, "Why are you waiting until you get home to ask me these questions?"

When she asked that, I finally understood that I had to ask questions when I was in the meeting—not wait until I got home. Because I had a good relationship with my school administrators, I knew they would welcome my questions just as I would welcome theirs. I no longer had to wait until I got home to hash out a situation with my wife, who was a third-party participant in the event. I was tired of not fully understanding what was going on with students in 'my' school. My heighted frustration over the issue is what made me push through this merge, and I remember the exact meeting when I finally used my voice. I was in a behavioral team meeting with several educators. The counselor started talking about a SIT Team meeting and the changes to a student's 504 plan. I looked at the counselor and said, "I have no clue what you are talking about, so I don't know how to help." It was at that moment where walls came down, and the educators laughed. We talked for a few minutes so that I could play catch up and get on the same page as everyone else. In the end, we all felt better about the situation, and I was able to give better input on what I could do to support both the student and staff members. Everyone understood that we weren't fighting each other, and the goal was the same. Now, we simply were communicating differently.

Another important thing for officers to remember is that talking to educators is very different from talking with other officers. For officers who frequently work in schools, you are probably in charge of talking with educators about their crisis plan or lockdown procedures. During these conversations or presentations, it is imperative that we mold our conversation to our audience. We must remember that our experiences in the field and/or training have most likely 'hardened' our perceptions of certain violent events. Much like those working in the medical field can talk about cutting patients open with ease, officers can often talk about violent situations with ease. One of the fastest ways to turn educators "off" to our message is to talk about being shot at, the blood and guts of an incident, or about the possibility of death in schools. Screaming and yelling or trying to scare educators into 'submission' with a 90-minute training isn't going to make them perform any better in a real-world situation. Understanding that talking in depth over lunch about the crime scene you went to last night isn't something most educators want to hear or view as 'cool.' Realizing that educators aren't wired to think that this kind of talk is 'normal' is a big step in crafting and communicating a message that will be heard and valued. When I speak to educators, I try to empower them by showing them how they can make the choices that will potentially save the lives of their students. The reality is that, as officers, we must soften our message when communicating with educators, and if that is not something you are comfortable with, or you're not sure if what you want to say is beneficial, it is always ok to ask the administrator before the topic is discussed. The goal is getting the information out there, not to scare or turn off our staff.

We have to remember that when we are in a school, we have something we don't have on the streets, and that is time. We also must remember that the important conversations we need to have, could and should happen PRIOR to an incident. I will talk about this more in the next chapter but understanding that we can better understand each other and be on the same page in front of students or parents by simply talking through situations before they occur, can do wonders when it comes to merging our worlds.

The View From the Educator's World:

504. IEP. SIT. GEI. ESL. ESI. SPED. PLC. PBIS.

The list can go on and on and on and on......

Edu jargon. You won't find a school and district (or state agency) that isn't built upon it. I won't lie—anytime we are implementing something new, I'm the first one in my school to create an acronym. These shortened phrases allow educators to communicate quickly and more effectively. As educators, we are cautious about how we use these acronyms in front of parents and other non-educators, and we make sure to fully explain ourselves and what the implications are behind each of these acronyms. Why then, do we not afford officers the same respect and opportunity?

Let's start with an incident that I'm sure is not completely unfamiliar to educators: a student attempting to leave the building. For me, this is always a call for an officer if I believe the student will actually leave. While students eloping is not uncommon in schools, sometimes there are disabilities or other circumstances that make a specific elopement situation different from others. I should note that I have never worked in an elementary school that had a designated officer on site. I have always had to call to ask for one to be dispatched when needed, which adds a significant amount of time before they arrive to aid in a situation. Sometimes, by the time they arrive, the situation is much calmer, and they are no longer needed. Sometimes, the situation has continued to escalate which leaves no time to communicate.

Back to the story: An elementary student is attempting to leave the building. This particular student had autism, and therefore, needed more time to communicate. The student was also extremely sensitive to touch and didn't like others in close proximity. This meant that our standard approach to prevent a student from leaving—using proximity or our bodies to block the exit—would not work and, in fact, would escalate the situation. When the officer arrived, the student was actively trying to leave and was about halfway out the front door. The officer (unaware of any of the above information) immediately went to use his body to move the student back inside the building. Was he restraining? No. But he was touching the student and using very direct verbal commands. Both of these actions instantly escalated the situation. I was behind the student and mouthed to the officer, "IEP for AU." He gave me a sideways glance, so I used my hands to make an A and a U in sign language. He looked at me like I had lost my mind. He had no idea what I was referring to, let alone what the implications were for either of those. Therefore, he could not adjust what he was doing to better support the student.

My normal method for communicating was out the window. If I would have mouthed that statement to any educator, they immediately would have understood that they needed to slow their speech, soften their tone, ask more questions, and position their body differently. It's not that the officer had done anything wrong at all, but at that moment he was making things worse and there wasn't anything I could do to help him or the student. I realized that in this moment, my only option was to tell the officer what I needed him to do. I told him I needed him to use a lower voice and him to take a step back.

Here's the clutch moment—because that officer had responded to my building before and he knew me, he trusted what I was saying and did what I asked. If it had been a new officer whom I had never worked with before, this approach would not have worked. None of us would appreciate being called to help and then told exactly what to do.

In the moment, it is never the appropriate or the best time to have the conversations about what is happening or who is involved—but sometimes we don't have a choice. The officer above might have understood and adjusted his approach if I had used the full word "autism" instead of the abbreviation; however, changing "IEP" to "individual education plan" would not have helped him at all. Officers do not take education classes, nor do they attend professional development where edu-jargon is used. It's one thing to know what the edu-jargon stands for, but something completely different to understand how each of these can dramatically change how each situation is addressed. As educators, it is okay to help the officers out a bit! In 95% of situations I've been involved in over the last 18 years, there have always been moments where I could have helped more than I did to make sure the officer had all of the information. In the situation above, it would have taken me less than 10 seconds to tell the officer that the student was very sensitive to touch and struggles with verbal communication before he engaged with the student, and to communicate that I only needed his support in case the student got out of the building.

Another aspect for educators to recognize is that officers and educators communicate differently nonverbally, as well. While things are fast paced in a school and educators will always want more time, we should always find time to communicate about student needs. Not all meetings are long, but we have the ability to connect quickly in the hallway and can say things like, "Joe is Handle-with-Care today." This simple phrase speaks a thousand words about the day Joe is going to have and, in turn, the day that all adults supporting Joe will have. When we don't have time to meet in person, we send emails and messages about what student needs a break, or a comment they made about something that happened last night at home. All of these moments allow educators to best support students throughout the day with every piece of information we have. Educators also have a variety of plans we can fall back on when students are struggling, and since we work with the same students every day, we can flush out these plans over time and change them as needed. Officers do not have this luxury. They are often dispatched to a call that they have no background information on, responding to students who they have never met before. When officers respond to calls at schools, you can almost sense their discomfort as they walk into the building. Oftentimes, none of their training has helped them understand how to talk to children, let alone children who are being aggressive, defiant, and unsafe.

The more I listened to John and understood the perspective of officers arriving to support calls at my building, the more appreciation I gained for their urgency in wanting to clear the scene. To this day, I giggle at the somewhat harsh language that officers use or how quickly an officer asks me, "So, are you all good here?" I used to take offense to that question and felt like they were rushing because they didn't find value in the work or didn't care, but that is not the case at all. I don't know if we can ever fully make officers feel comfortable in schools, especially when they only have a limited amount of time to clear the call and move on to the next. However, switching my perspective and thought process has allowed me to not judge in these moments, and be more direct with what I need. If I need an officer to wait until a parent has arrived, I specifically say that. If I need them to sit in on the conversation, I say that. If I don't, I tell them thank you for helping before they ask if they can leave. I also make sure to let them know where the staff bathroom is and offer a bottle of water or a granola bar if I have one, as well. Some officers that respond more frequently to my building now know where the candy dish is, and they feel comfortable enough to grab some without asking. Those moments show that we are communicating better, even though our languages will always be different.

The Merge:

Effective communication seems so simple, but it is the foundation on which all other merges are built. Educators and officers are equally responsible for helping each other in this area. The first step is to ask questions when you don't understand and give each other the grace to make sure that both parties have the appropriate and needed information to be helpful. This is easiest if you have the same team of educators and officers working together. If you have that luxury, then you can make this mutual agreement with one another. We also suggest and highly recommend that you designate a weekly time to meet together to clear the air of any negative interactions, debrief any big situations that happened, and bring each other up to speed on any new changes, students, or situations. If you don't have the same team of officers and educators consistently working together, then you should know to ask these questions individually. As I mentioned, I have never had an officer based in any building I've worked in; while there was always one officer who was assigned to respond to calls, they only responded about 50% of the time. I say this to discourage you from putting down the book with an excuse of "I don't have an officer assigned to my building and someone different always responds." The work is too important to stop at Chapter 1 with such an excuse.

As a school-based officer, it is important to remember that we are all on the same team. Educators speak a different language and experience different emotions than officers do. This is why programs are met with such high praise from law enforcement but have mixed reviews from the educators. Understanding that we have time to slow a situation down and have a conversation in 'plain speak' with educators creates the foundation to a successful relationship. As school-based officers, we obviously don't have to know everything about education, just like we don't expect educators to know everything about law enforcement. In any situation, it is okay to ask questions in an educational setting. By having a better, well-rounded understanding of both languages, we better serve our schools, students, and communities.

Finally, remember that while we have the same goal of keeping students and our schools safe, sometimes we go about it in different ways. As educators, when you call for an officer to assist in a situation, you have invited them in. With that, you must take their perspective, training, and voice into consideration. Just like all educators have different experiences and training that guide their work, so do officers. An officer arriving at a school being told a student is eloping has one thing on their mind—get the student back in the building. Whether or not the student had an IEP did not change the fact that if they left the building, they could be seriously injured. As educators, we often think of the emotional aspects first, and the physical aspects second. Officers tend to be the opposite of this. By just that alone, we will approach situations differently. To successfully accomplish this merge, both sides will have to focus on this work during every interaction. Like any change, it will get easier over time and with each situation that is worked through. As we stated in the introduction, we hope that after each chapter you take time to pause, reflect, and adjust your professional practice. As we move into the next four merges, we believe they are only possible if effective communication remains a focal point.

Discussion/Thinking Points:

- Educators: Think of a time when an officer responded to a situation that you were involved in. Where did the communication break down?
- Educators: How might you be intentional in clarifying moments in conversations?
- Educators: Remember that you need to lead the conversation or encounter. It's your building and your students. If you have a question, ask. If you have a need, say it.
- Officers: Take advantage of having time in a school. Where can you find moments to intentionally pause and make sure everyone in the room is on the same page?

● Officers: If you don't know what the edu-jargon means, don't be afraid to ask! Avoid using police codes/signals and just use "plain speak" to get the point or options across.

CHAPTER 2

Addressing Student
Behavior

Working through addressing student behaviors is the second merge that must occur between the two worlds, as this is most likely when the majority of our interactions will take place. Again, this might change based on your specific situation and whether or not you have officers assigned directly to your building. However, the clash between our worlds when addressing student behaviors is astronomical, and if not merged completely, it has the potential to significantly damage professional relationships. Why is this one so difficult? When we began working together to attack this merge, we realized that oftentimes educators have strong emotions relating to student consequences, or lack thereof. In the officer's world, things are more often viewed in black and white—in that, they are trained to believe that any infraction should be met with the same consequence. When officers enter schools and are met with a myriad of potential consequences, both worlds can become frustrated and confused, and left questioning if their professional opinion was valued.

This merge came to light around our dinner table as we shared our frustrations over how situations were handled by the other world. As we continued to work through this and share different perspectives, we both realized we didn't understand the other's viewpoint and/or policies. Without effective communication, however, this merge stands little chance of occurring. Both sides must foster and embrace open conversations around student behavior to clarify what options are on the table compared to what policies must be enforced. If you find yourself working through this alone, we will offer considerations for each side at the end of the chapter that you can take into your practice to alleviate frustrations and confusions.

Again, this chapter is not made to supersede any internal policies and or procedures that you have put in place. We understand that this can be a very broad topic, but we have chosen to address how these incidents unfolded in our world. Officers get told that we should stay out of school rules, which is absolutely true. However, educators must remember that officers want to be present to offer support in situations that happen in schools. While reading this chapter, it is important to remember that federal laws have addressed when and how law enforcement can be brought into situations at the school level. Both sides must approach addressing student behaviors with these in mind so that neither side oversteps or inadvertently causes more problems.

The View from the Officer's World:

As a School Resource Officer (SRO), I found that student behavior was a tricky world to live in. While we strive to be a part of the school community and culture, and want to build relationships with staff and students, sometimes we have to go into "law enforcement mode." This can sometimes cause confusion from staff and students as well as create angst in our own hearts. As officers, we understand the potential unattended consequences when we arrest a student or a parent. Relationships that take years to build are so quickly broken between the officer, the student(s), the parents, and sometimes even the educators. When addressing student behavior, sometimes there is confusion as to why the officer acted in a certain way or why the officer seemed to not act at all.

After starting my first School Resource Officer position, one of the first conversations I remember having with the high school principal was the two of us trying to hash out what he felt my role should look like versus what I thought my role should look like. I had never been an SRO before, but I would be the third SRO he had worked with in his career. He was drawing upon past experiences, and I was fighting to make sure we started the relationship correctly. One of the things that we agreed on was that I would not be involved in violations of school rules. It is important for educators to know that if there is a "no hat policy" in the school, and I see Johnny with a hat on, I have no consequences to give him because that is not my role. So, if I tell Johnny to take his hat off, and he tells me to kick rocks, my hands are tied as to any kind of response. As an SRO, I didn't hand out detentions or suspensions. My consequences were legal only. To this day, I encourage SROs to help support as much as possible, especially if you have a good relationship with a student. However, don't muddy the waters as to why you are actually in the school. I didn't want or expect the principal to arrest a student or issue a citation, so in turn, my hope was that they didn't expect me to deal with gum, cellphones, or other school rule violations.

Let's say we are working together to tackle a situation in which a student violated a school rule, but it does involve us due to safety. It is important for officers to understand that inside of a school, there are a lot of consequences an administrator can assign. Sometimes those consequences are mandated, sometimes they vary based on the situation or totality of the circumstances. Whatever happens, that is really none of our concern because even if there is a school consequence, it doesn't affect the law enforcement consequence. It is also important to note that in a lot of cases, officers have three directions we can go: we can arrest, issue a citation/notice to appear, or give a verbal/written warning. The most important thing for officers to take from this chapter is that we must be as consistent as possible. For example, if Billy and Bobby get caught vaping in the bathroom for the third time, they should each receive the same consequence from the officer. On the school end, there might be variances based on how many times this has happened or the ages of Billy or Bobby, but officers should always strive to stay consistent.

Another aspect to consider for officers is the amount of time we actually have when working on situations in schools. On the streets, we don't always have time as a luxury. In schools, we have time to talk things out with students, with staff, and with administrators. Before the situation above arose, administrators and I had spent time during one of our weekly meetings discussing what would happen if a student was to be found in possession of an illegal narcotic. We agreed that if that happened, I would arrest the student(s) and take them to Juvenile Intake. It didn't matter if it was the star running back on the football team or the tuba player in the marching band (GO SOUSAPHONES)— the legal consequence would always be the same. Agreeing upon this was important because it took any "favoritism" out of the equation. Jenny got a vaping ticket because that is what we do with all first-time offenders, not because Jenny is a 4.0 student. For officers, it's not that we must justify our decisions to anyone, and truly most consequences can't be legally aired for juveniles. However, as we know with working in schools, EVERYONE talks, so the consequence will get around one way or the other. When the parents of the student have a question, we can fall back on our consistent policies and procedures and ensure there is no instance where one student was treated differently than the other. Take advantage of having the time and the space to have conversations with administrators before situations happen. You will most likely find that once they understand that you will be consistent with your consequences every time, administrators will have your back and help explain this to parents.

I also used time to my advantage when interviewing students. On the streets, if I thought a child committed a crime, I had no choice but to intervene without a parent or guardian present. However, in schools, if a student was suspected of committing a crime, I called the parents first because most of the time, I'd have hours to work though the situation. This helped create trust between myself and the community. I was not trying to 'get one over' on the student by tricking them. It was evident that I wanted their parents to be there so they could hear the same report as I was hearing in real time. This also aligned with school policy, which required a parent be notified when law enforcement was going to speak to their child. Sometimes the parents could make it to the school, sometimes we had to meet off-site, and sometimes, simply having the parents on speakerphone satisfied all parties. For officers, I urge you to know if the school or district you are in has a policy similar to this so that you are aware before a situation occurs.

While it's always best to discuss a situation before acting, sometimes that's just not feasible because we don't live in a perfect world. Again, using time to our benefit can really help all parties grow from the situation. As an example, during a school dance, a student alerted myself and the assistant principal that they believed another student was intoxicated. I knew who the student was, and the assistant principal and I were in agreement that I would bring her into his office so we could work through the situation in a more private setting away from the other students. When I approached her, she was mouthing to her friends that she was taking "shots, shots, shots." When she saw me, she immediately stopped dancing and stood frozen. We walked back to the assistant principal's office, and I immediately smelled an odor that I knew to be consumed alcohol. Now, I could go on for a few pages with all the legal jargon, and how I was trained to write my report explaining my training, knowledge, and experience. However, believe me when I say, I knew she had been drinking. We called her parents and had them head to the school. She had no alcohol containers on her person and admitted to the assistant principal that she had been drinking at home before having someone drive her to the dance. I realized that the administration and I had never actually had the conversation about what to do when we discovered an underage student had been consuming alcohol off-campus but was intoxicated on-campus. As an officer, I had two options: arrest her and take her to juvenile intake or issue her a notice to appear. The assistant principal also had a number of things he could do. At that moment, I realized that there would most likely be two separate consequences— One would be legal and one from the school. Yes, there can be a school AND a legal consequence within the same situation. While standing in the office, I called a 'time-out' and had the assistant principal exit the office with me. We stood outside his door, so we could still see and hear anything that was going on inside his office; however, I needed to make sure we were both on the same page. It took around 45 seconds for me to explain what I could do, and what I thought would be the best option at the time. Now, ultimately, it was my decision as to what to do, and I wasn't asking for any kind of permission. I was simply providing a space where we could share and gain insight to get on the same page. This served as a great reminder that we are all on the same team. We both wanted to keep the school safe, and we both had different ways to do it. When the parents arrived at school, we talked through the situation as well as the legal and school consequences for their daughter's actions. This was as much of a success as we could gather from this situation. Was it a success that we had an intoxicated student on campus at a dance? No. However, we showed the students that we were a team, and that we were both there to support all students, while ensuring we did what was necessary to keep the school safe. I strived to have every situation end as a positive; however, sometimes that didn't happen.

When I first started as an SRO, I had a major learning moment. There was a fight in the school and two students were taken to the office. When I walked by and saw the students, I simply asked, "What happened?" One of the students didn't even acknowledge me, while the other student responded with, "We fought." About that time, the administrator asked me to step into the office with him while he talked with one of the students. I saw no problem with it. Technically, there was mutual battery, or at the very least, disorderly conduct, so I had a legal reason to be there. In my head, there wasn't gross bodily injury to either student, so I was not thinking about doing anything legal unless something larger arose from the situation. I was simply there to be a fly on the wall and to make sure things didn't get out of control in the office. The first student came in and was respectful, answered all the questions that were asked, admitted wrongdoing and apologized. He was given a school consequence, the administrator called his parents, and he went about his day. The second student was the complete opposite. He was rude, condescending, and difficult. Again, I was only there because I happened to have been walking by the office. The student was able to get under the skin of the administrator, and it took me by surprise when the administrator looked at me and said, *"Well, fighting is illegal so go ahead and arrest him and take him to jail. I'm done with him."* This put me in a very difficult situation. With it being my first year, I didn't really know what to do. I needed to back the administrator to show that we were a team, but I wasn't going to arrest one student and not the other. Really, I wasn't going to arrest either, regardless of whether the administrator wanted me to or not. Again, I had time, and I used it by again calling a 'time-out.' We had the student sit back out in the main office, and I was able to talk with the administrator one-on-one. I explained that I was not going to arrest anyone for a mutual fight at school unless something else illegal came out. I explained that him yelling at me in anger to arrest the student was not going to solve any situation. We took some time to get back on the same page so that we could solve the problem and not fight each other. We had the student return, and I explained that there could be legal consequences for fighting; however, we (the administrator and I) believed that learning could take place with a school consequence and the situation would not be repeated. With calmer heads prevailing, the student was able to call his parents, receive his school consequence, and go about his day. Even in this learning situation, there were positives that emerged because we paused and used effective communication. The administrator and I were able to work through a situation and strengthen our working relationship. Everyone involved was able to see that I was there to support, and that ultimately, I wanted to make sure I could justify my actions and defend what I did to keep the school safe.

Both of these situations were based on legal interventions with compliant students, but we all know that is not always the case. The first big, eye-opening situation that I encountered as an SRO occurred while I was walking down the hall in one of the elementary schools. I heard a loud commotion and saw my first ever classroom evacuation; approximately 20 first-grade students exited their classroom and walked calmly to an adjoining (or 'buddy') classroom. When I walked into the doorway of the original classroom, I saw this little six-year-old boy jumping from desk to desk, kicking and breaking things in the process. He hopped down off of a desk, walked to the teacher's desk, and began throwing things and smashing things on the ground. In my big-boy cop voice, I sternly said, "Hey! Stop that!" I will never forget when the six-year-old looked right at me, gave me the two middle finger salute, and continued with his destruction. I was shocked. This little boy wasn't going to do as I said? Now what? Was I going to physically intervene in the situation? No, he was six and only doing property damage. What else could I do? I could create a report for Child in Need of Care and list the teacher as the victim of property damage. I could put an estimate cost for the damage, and do my best to see that the family of the student would have to reimburse the teacher. I saw the administrator and other members of his team go over and guide the student to a 'calm down room.' I walked back over to the teacher and explained the process and that I would just need an estimate of everything that was broken. I was in absolute awe when the teacher told me that she did not want a report taken, nor the student's family to pay her back for damages. I was confused, and honestly, upset that any of my 'power' was taken away from me. There was nothing I could do to help this situation. I stood by feeling helpless, which was a weird feeling. I had no 'victim' and therefore, had no crime to report. When I got home and had time to talk with Heather, I told her how frustrated I was with the fact that there was really nothing I could do because the teacher didn't want my help. Heather laughed at me and told me that I didn't want to know the amount of money she spent out of our pocket to replace items that a student had intentionally broken. While I didn't have a conversation with my elementary school administrator about how often situations like this happen, it was nice to realize that most teachers understand that a relationship with a student and his/her family is usually more important than monetary reimbursement for minor items. For officers reading this, I urge you to pause when helping with situations and be prepared for educators to not want to file reports and be listed as the victim. It does not mean they do not want your help or value what you can do. Most educators simply view these incidents as part of their job.

This situation actually led to a separate factor I had not considered. I was asked by the Superintendent during a leadership team meeting if I wanted to go be trained in MANDT. Using my new communication skills from merge one, I felt very comfortable stating out loud that I didn't know what MANDT was. After some chuckles, again not at me, but at the situation, he explained that MANDT is a training for student holds. Now, I want to be clear that what I am about to say is in no way a slight to MANDT or any other student hold program; however, I was in no way interested in that type of training. I had my own restraint training in the police academy and participated in yearly training ever since. I am not a fan of officers being trained in any student-hold training. The reason is fairly simple. When I enter a physical situation, everything I have on my duty belt, my ankle, my vest, etc., enters the situation with me. That seems like a 'duh' moment, but let's really think about it. If there is an out of control 10-year-old, and I enter the situation to participate and hold the student, and that 10-year-old grabs for my gun (either intentionally or unintentionally), I have just escalated the situation. All my restraint training and self-defense tactics that I have been taught have taken into account having these tools on my person. I have been trained for hundreds of hours, to the point where it is almost second nature. If I were to be trained in a different approach, that would potentially muddy the waters and would not be beneficial in any way. This means that for most situations, I responded but did not intervene. After a conversation at our dinner table one night, I realized that what seemed simple to me, probably needed to be said out loud. I made a point to speak at our next building safety meetings to explain why I would not physically intervene in situations unless it was life or death, or a situation I believed the staff could not control. I was able to explain to administration and staff the dire consequences of a student getting my firearm or taser, or even a baton. Again, just taking the time that we were afforded, it was amazing how we were able to get on the same page and have a better understanding of the work each other did. This helped as we addressed a lot of our student behaviors in the future because we had taken the time to understand the role that the other party played.

Once we had a handle on what to do to address student behaviors that occurred inside of the schools, I realized that there was still more to this merge. For example, there are some situations that bubble inside of a school that do not have any school consequences because they happened off school property. The school is simply involved because that is the easiest/best place to find the student. In my experience, the most common situation was when students would send each other inappropriate photos while at home, but administration was then notified at the school. Now, I won't spend too much time on this point, as that merge is quite simple. We are still in the administrator's school. They have the right to know that something is going on in their school; however, it could be as simple as, "*I'm going to call this student's parents because of something that happened at home last night, and the parent may be showing up. This doesn't have anything to do with the school, but if anything changes, I will let you know.*" Having the trust and the relationship to understand that working together does not always mean we will be working collaboratively still allows us to be a united front. Letting administrators know that parents may be coming to the school, and it has nothing to do with them or the school, goes a long way in building that trust. I also would start my conversations with the parents or guardians with, "*This is something that happened outside of school and doesn't involve the school. They don't know anything other than you are here, and there won't be any school consequences unless this spills out into disrupting the school day.*" Being the only SRO for the district, it was reassuring to the school, the community, and honestly, to myself to know that these types of situations would all be handled the same way because I was the one handling them.

Finally, it is important to remember that everyone who responds to incidents in a school must be on the same page. In talking with educators, I learned that often times their anxiety increases when situations are handled differently depending on which officer responds. Again, everyone will have their own way of responding to calls for support. However, we must work to ensure that we are addressing student behaviors in a consistent manner so that the school and the community know that we are on the same team. Also, it isn't a bad thing to ask educators, or the officer who is normally assigned to the building, how they would normally handle the situation. These minor shifts in practice can make a huge impact in the relationship we have with students and educators.

The View from The Educator's World:

Addressing student behaviors in schools is embedded in our work every day. Many school districts have a behavior consequence plan that has been adopted by the local Board of Education. If not, districts and schools typically have some form of written hierarchy that outlines consequences that match the severity of the behavior. Certain behaviors should be addressed in the classroom, while some behaviors filter up to the office for administration to address—and a few are severe enough that the district or local Board of Education assigns consequences. However, there are typically many consequence options listed for each behavior or level of behavior. This is because there are always multiple factors to consider, resulting in behavior systems in a constant "grey" area. Children (anyone under the age of 18) will always find new ways to stump us, and while I won't go into the multitude of behavior modification theories, know that schools are ever-changing and always evolving when it comes to addressing student behaviors.

When I think back to my experiences in school, I cannot remember any instances of a classmate exhibiting explosive or unsafe behavior. For many adults, this is also the case. Students with extreme disabilities were often not placed in general education classrooms. The struggle many of us now face is that we welcome all students into general education classrooms, and we must add various daily supports to meet their needs. For students in today's classrooms, it is not uncommon to evacuate a classroom or hear very aggressive language. These extreme behaviors are often what prompts administrators to call officers to a school. However, this is where things can go awry—and quickly.

Let's dive deeper into what this might look like, and why this issue was brought up around our dinner table. Like many educators, I have had my fair share of injuries from students. Some were completely unintentional, such as when I was head-butted by a student who had autism. I've also been injured by students who were so overloaded with sensory input, or frustrated by their lack of control, that they honestly were not able to think. In those moments, I and other staff members have been injured as we tried to support the student(s) best while they are in their altered state. However, there have been a few students who were intentionally trying to harm staff. Now, it is important to understand that while the intent of the student was to harm, I believe there are always underlying factors or trauma (some we know may about, and some we don't) that cause big actions to come out of small bodies. At the middle and high school levels, students are also often processing stress, anxiety, and bullying. My point is that sometimes, students are aggressive with staff or other students intentionally, and when that happens, we must intervene. These interventions are designed to give the student space, time, and options if possible. We typically only intervene further if property damage will be high, or if there is a risk of self-harm to the student or others. Again, I have never worked in a school with a set SRO, which means there is often travel time involved for support to arrive during a situation. When a student escalates to the point that staff must intervene, I always make a call for an officer (and the guardian of the student).

So, when staff are intervening with the student and the officer arrives, the ideal scenario is actually for someone from the family to arrive and help calm the student down—but sometimes, that doesn't happen. Every time an officer would arrive to provide support, they would stand in the doorway or hallway (or wherever we were) and watch as the student punched, kicked, bit, threw items, etc. Staff members would leave with broken bones, teeth marks, bleeding scratch marks, and muscle injuries. The officer would help locate a guardian, occasionally stay until they arrived, and then leave with little conversation. Staff involved would first see the school nurse to assess injuries, then come to my office where we would complete injury reports and send anyone who needed further medical attention to the local clinic. In our exhausted state, frustrations continued to run high. Why would an officer just stand there and watch us get beaten up? Why should we call them if they aren't going to do anything to help?

I had no answers. Unfortunately, I joined in the conversation with staff and shared my frustrations over how little support the officers offered, time and time again. For perspective, did we call for an officers' support every day? Of course not. In my many years as an educator, I have had students with significant struggles who required support multiple times a week, but that was typically not the case. Everyone's experiences will be different with students who have aggressive behavior, and I will not attempt to generalize. I can speak with certainty, that every time I have been involved in a situation with a highly aggressive student, the emotions from all staff are high. It is emotional to see a student in that state and know that there's not a lot we can do to help, plus there's the added stress of keeping everyone safe.

One day, my frustration overflowed, and it landed at our dinner table conversation. John was a great husband and listened intently. When I was finished, he simply asked, "Can I tell you why officers are not intervening?" Stunned, I looked at him and waited because I was sure there wasn't going to be any valid reason given. He went on to explain that when an officer enters any scene, they are also entering everything they have on them into the situation. For example, if they have any form of weapon, handcuffs, car keys, radio ... it can now be grabbed by the student and potentially escalate the situation even more.

It got better. John went on to ask me what it was that an officer hadn't done that I wished they would have, aside of physically intervening. Again, I didn't have an answer. Did I want them to arrest the student? No. Did I want them to yell and scream? No. The truth was that we were all just tired of getting hurt, clearing the classrooms, and the emotional rollercoaster that went along with it. There wasn't anything that anyone could do to make that reality different, so why was I mad at the officer? I had never considered this, and to this day, I wish that I had been in a calm enough state to ask this of the many officers whom I had interacted with over the years. When I think of the multiple professional relationships that have been damaged over this, it makes me so sad. The next day I went back and called an immediate crisis team meeting to make sure they understood these points as well. While it doesn't make it easier for us in the moment, it does make sense. We could now change our views of the officers and begin to communicate more clearly about what we needed in each situation.

Things look differently now. When we call for an officer, I make sure that we know what we need them to help us with. If we cannot articulate that, then we don't make the call. This was a subtle change in our practice at the school, and we never really communicated this shift to the officers. We simply changed our practice. You might be wondering if it made a difference, and it did on both sides. Officers actually have stated they enjoy responding to our building now, because if we call, they know that we really need support, and we will tell them what we need. Sometimes they will even call us directly while en route to see if we need help locating a parent, a home visit, or if they need to respond directly to the school. Our crisis team also has a visible respect for the officers when they respond, and everyone on the team now feels comfortable and confident to say exactly what is needed when they arrive. This helps speed the call up as well, because everyone is empowered to help.

For those who are fortunate to have officers assigned to your building, or have the same officer who typically responds, it is important to understand that we cannot use them as a threat. When a student is refusing to comply, being disrespectful, unsafe, or making threats, do not throw out "I'll just call for an officer and let them deal with you." Mean what you say, and say what you mean. Do not try to trick students into changing their behavior by threatening to call an officer. At the end of the day, if you call an officer and no law is being broken, what do you want the officer to do if the student still doesn't comply? I get it; I've been there. I've sat in the hallway with students who sit down and refuse to move. I've followed students as they walked about the building for hours, refusing to be in class. I've been on the playground with students who refuse to come inside. Staff have urged me to call an officer because "We don't have time for to babysit." And they are right—but the question becomes, "*What is the officer going to do?*" They can't arrest the student for sitting down, or refusing to be in their classroom. If an officer is called, I have now put them in a horrible situation. When they arrive, they can attempt to scare the student into complying with their presence, but is that really what I want? This does nothing but teach students that officers are scary and that they only come when you are bad. In middle and high schools, involving an officer when there isn't a reason teaches students that officers are only there to enforce laws, not to problem solve and be another trusted adult.

Is it all sunshine and roses? No, we are continually growing and learning from each other. Like any professional relationship, there are ups and downs each time we tackle new situations. In multiple buildings I've worked in, students have made choices that have resulted in expulsion. These behaviors are typically also illegal, which adds another element to navigate. For example, a student brings a weapon to school or makes a significant threat. As a school administrator, these are calls for an officer every time because not only did the student break a school rule, but they also broke the law. What I have learned from these situations is that this is often not the time to have the community view officers as "'just a support for the school." There will be a school consequence and a separate legal consequence. As an administrator, I begin making that as clear as I can as soon as the student's guardian(s) arrive. Most of the time, the officers are in the room when this happens, and I make it clear to the family that we are only discussing school consequences. I then explain that because the student broke the law, we had to also call for an officer, and they will then speak to the legal consequences. This is critical because while the school or district often has a wide array of options that can be assigned, officers typically do not have leniency.

So how do we work together in these regards? First, once we ensure that everyone is safe, we can pause and have a conversation with each other to ensure clarity. We can take a few minutes to restate the situation as it happened, making sure everyone understands the facts. We can also talk about the options that we have on the table, and how similar situations in the past have been addressed. This ensures that both the officers and administrators can talk through their plan. Sometimes the plans might overlap (like creating a safety plan for the student) and can include information that is needed if the student does have charges filed. Pausing and taking time to have these conversations is invaluable in making sure that we collaborate effectively, while doing what makes the most sense in each situation. Second, as an administrator, it is our role to help preserve the relationship between the family and the officer. We can do this by helping the family get in contact with the police department when they have further questions or by helping explain the process the best we can. We must remember that this is often a scary time for families, and they will feel more comfortable talking with staff they know at the school rather than trying to call a police department. We are not legal counsel and should never offer advice, but for any student who is facing legal consequences, we can offer support to the family.

For educators, we must make sure we are not ever putting officers in a bad position by expecting them to be involved in non-legal behavior situations. They can absolutely support us, and you would be hard pressed to find an officer who did not want to help. However, it is not our responsibility to speak about legal consequences or use their presence as a threat to students or families. We also have to remember to take the time to pause and talk out situations whenever possible, so we can ensure everyone can act in the best interest of all students and the school as a whole.

The Merge:

Addressing student behavior in schools requires the use of the effective communication skills we discussed in the first chapter. One of the main merges we advocate for with student behavior is to always take the time to process the situation together before acting. Very few behaviors must be addressed without first being able to pause and have a conversation. This conversation allows both parties to share their perspectives and plans, ensuring that everyone is on the same page and feels comfortable with how to proceed. We must hold space and understand that while we each come from different worlds, and we have different courses of action for addressing student behavior, we can still merge to do what is best for students and staff.

There is rarely a time where a crime committed on school grounds does not result in both a school and legal consequence. It is important to work together during the investigation so that both sides know what is going on and everyone has all the facts. This again relies on constant communication and effectively using the time that is available. Knowing that these types of situations can cause a lot of fear for the student and guardian, it is important for educators to answer questions pertaining to school consequences and stay away from legal justification. Likewise, it is important for officers to provide answers regarding the legal ramifications of the situation while leaving school consequences to the educators. It is also important that we continue to ask each other questions and state what we need from the other. We must demonstrate mutual respect and maintain clear boundaries so that students, staff, and the community understand that while our mission is the same—**keeping our schools safe**—sometimes we must address things separately.

> *As an educator, it is our responsibility to use officers as a resource when we really need them to support and help and not as the 'scary enforcer' of all the school rules.*

As an educator, it is our responsibility to use officers as a resource when we really need them to support and help and not as the 'scary enforcer' of all the school rules. Having clarity yourself as to what this looks like, as well as helping staff understand their role, is essential to preserving the relationship with all stakeholders. As an officer it is important to note that our presence in every situation may not be warranted. Instead, we must trust the relationship we have built and know that if there is or was a crime committed, educators will use their best judgment to get us involved, if and when necessary. Sometimes, a situation at school is simply that—a situation at school, and we can continue to give high-fives and go about our day.

Discussion/Thinking Points:

- Educators: Before you call for an officer to support you with student behavior, think of what it is that you want them to do. When they arrive, be very direct in what support you are needing. Officers cannot read your minds.
- Educators: Are your staff clear on what the scope and role of the officer are?
- Educators: How might you support Officers in preserving the relationships with families in difficult times?
- Officers: Is your role in the school clear to the educators that you support?
- Officers have different ways to handle the same problem, BUT for consistency and fairness, every situation should be handled the same way, no matter the student.
- Officers can go hands-on in a situation; however, doing so brings in a multitude of other safety concerns. How better can an officer support staff in a difficult situation?
- Officers and Educators: Make sure you are spending the time to thoroughly talk through a situation so that both sides are clear on what the other is doing and why. Use time to your advantage.

CHAPTER 3

Policies Around Children in Need

There is probably nothing more emotional or heartbreaking for an educator than to listen to a child of any age share horrible living conditions or allegations of abuse. First, we typically have a pretty solid relationship with the student if they feel safe enough to share something so serious. This means that we have an emotional investment in the well-being of that particular child. Second, we are somewhat powerless in helping the child. Education, by nature, is a professional field in which we help others learn in some form or fashion. When we can't do anything to help, it raises even more emotional tension. John will joke that this merge is still one that Heather can't fully embrace because her emotional brain takes over, and there is very little logic being used. All she sees is a child who is hurting, and she has to send them back into that environment—even after the child trusted her to help.

On the flip side, this is probably one of the worst calls that officers must respond to. When going into a house, we get to experience the life of the child(ren) inside the home. We see the living conditions; we can smell the musty air; we dig through layers of trash to get from the front door to the living room. All the while, in the back of our head, we understand that we can't judge what a person or family is going through at the time. Is this the living condition I would want my child to grow up in? No, but is it my job to make the decision to remove a child from the home because it is not what I would want for my child? Also, no. When we enter a school as an officer, a lot of people joke that we are "kiddie cops" or "kindergarten cops." This is funny because yes, we do a lot of fun things with students. We get to read to them, play dodgeball, and give high fives in the hallways. But what others don't see is that when you work in the schools, every call that comes in now involves a child. Every abuse case involves a child. This weighs very heavy on our hearts. Sometimes it is hard to not lead with our hearts and emotions, but our job is to put those aside and lead with what the letter of the law states.

Does this merge look different at different age levels of the child? Absolutely. A five-year-old sharing information is very different from a 16-year-old sharing information. Does this merge look different depending on the socio-economic area? Absolutely not. Heather's heart has led her to love working in underserved communities, but she has also worked in very affluent communities. In each district, no matter what city or area, the stories of abuse and neglect are similar. Furthermore, our own children go to school in an affluent school district and hearing the stories that our children share with us around our dinner table about the struggles their friends are going through, demonstrates that there is no economic variation amongst children who sometimes find themselves in tough situations.

Before we get too deep into this merge, we want to acknowledge that each state, district, department, etc. will likely have their own procedures surrounding reporting of children in need of care. We in no way wish to start a conversation that questions those policies or procedures because they exist for a reason. As we work through this merge, our goal is to offer considerations to help protect the relationships between educators and officers and shed some insight into the perspective of their respective worlds.

The View from the Officer's World:

Thirteen years into this work, and I still have to sleep on the couch because of this merge. This is the hardest topic to merge worlds on, but it is in the trenches that an amazing relationship can blossom.

Before you read on, remember to never give up and never stop fighting. But before there are words, we must remember that we are on the same side, and we are fighting the problem together—NOT each other. I wish there was something easy that I could say, or a magic wand we could wave to make this topic go away. I even contemplated trying to take this chapter out of the book, but we don't run away from difficult situations. As Heather will say, "We can do hard things." While I acknowledge that this is a hard topic, it is probably one of the more important ones when it comes to getting on the same page and at least seeing the other world in our conversations.

This will be a short chapter for me, as unfortunately, there is only so much legally officers can do to try and smooth this over. Heather will say that this is hard for educators because they lead with their heart. This is true. They have a vested interest in the students in their school. When educators refer to the students as "their kids," they mean it. This is not saying that officers don't care about the kids. I still run into my "kiddos" who will call me Officer John, even though I haven't been their SRO in six years! I care and love each of the kiddos I had the pleasure of spending time with during my time in the schools. The issue is, that while we do in fact have a heart, officers have been taught from the academy that we have to compartmentalize a lot about our feelings during an encounter. We must remain impartial and go where the facts take us.

There are set policies and procedures in handling reports of abuse and neglect that, unfortunately, have to be followed. This keeps checks and balances in order. For starters, we must remember that both educators and officers are mandated reporters to local Child Protective Services (CPS). This may be called something different depending on your state or jurisdiction, but when we say CPS, feel free to call it what you are used to. There are very few cases where officers can bypass these other agencies and immediately put a child in Police Protective Custody (PPC). Honestly, there is a good reason for that not being what we jump to initially. While there may be times that officers want to act, we simply do not have the legal backing to do so. This doesn't mean the work stops or that we just move on to the next call. In most jurisdictions, officers cannot remove a child and place them in PPC unless we feel the child is being put in imminent danger. That is an extremely high threshold, as it should be, to remove a child from a guardian's custody. So, as an officer, what else can we do?

As an SRO, I had monthly meetings with our social services and CPS agencies. It was good to talk about situations, hear concerns or repeat reports, and work together to provide services or resources to families so our children might flourish in an environment with loving, caring family members. Regrettably, looking back, I did not include the school as much as I should have. Providing a space to hear how the child was behaving in a school environment could have provided more clarity on the situation. If you have the opportunities to engage in this work, I highly encourage you to take full advantage. I was welcomed with open arms as a new voice to the team.

Throughout my work—and around my dinner table—I have experienced how deeply educators care for their students. I joke with a former superintendent that she is the reason I don't give out my cell phone number to people anymore. On more than one occasion, she would call me at three in the morning. I would roll over, slide the phone on, and muster up a, "Hello?" She would answer me by talking as if it was 10 in the morning, and she had just finished her third cup of coffee. She would explain that she was worried about a student, most of the time in elementary or middle school, who was talking about not having clean clothes or enough food at home. She wanted me to do a welfare check on the home for the safety of the child. Of course, I would conduct a welfare check on the home; however, did it warrant a 3:00 a.m. wakeup call? Not to mention the subsequent conversation I had to have with Heather about why a woman was calling me at 3:00 a.m. But, for the Superintendent—yes—she could not sleep knowing a student might not be okay.

In another instance, I had a principal call me 10 minutes before dismissal (which is when most student behaviors would happen, right?). He told me he had a student who stated he was scared to go home. I asked him why the student was scared, and the principal told me the student was afraid of his dad. When I arrived, the buses were getting ready to be loaded. I pulled the student into the office where I could talk with him one on one, and he explained that he wasn't going to get on the bus to go home because he was afraid of his dad. When I asked him why he was afraid, the student went into a story about how he was playing video games in the morning and didn't get any of his morning chores done before getting on the bus to come to school. When he was walking out of the front door, his dad asked if he had done his chores, and the student was honest and said that he hadn't. The student then proceeded to tell me that his dad told him that when he got off the bus, he would not have any fun because he would have to do all his chores as well as more "punishment chores." He said he was afraid of what the punishment chores were. When I asked if he had done punishment chores before and what those were, he said that he would have to hand wash dishes or scrub the baseboards around the living room. I asked a few more questions, but they all came out the same: the student didn't want to go home because of the fear of a punishment, not because of any physical fear. I told the student that he needed to get on the bus, or we would have to have his dad come pick him up from school. Ultimately, the student got on the bus, and I was able to talk with the principal about the interview. We were both relieved that the student was physically okay and that he was just worried about being punished. The principal called the father to talk to him, and while I didn't hear the other side of the phone call, both parties were laughing. I checked in with the student the next day, and he told me that his dad made him do some extra chores, but they "weren't as bad as I thought."

I don't share these stories to make light of abuse or neglect reports from students. This also doesn't mean I have never had to remove a child from the home. I think if you are in law enforcement, and especially, the SRO career long enough, you are going to have to make the decision to remove a child. I still remember the first time I removed a child. He was 16 years old, and asked to talk to me and the counselor. I had a decent relationship with him, and we would joke around in the hallways from time to time. I could tell by the look on his face and his expressions, that this was not one of those times. He told us that he was having a hard time at home and at school. No one thing in particular stood out, but he reported just a feeling of not being able to find joy. He wasn't being bullied, but he just couldn't find happiness in any of his friendships anymore. He told me he just wanted to "end it all." When I asked what he meant by that, he matter-of-factly stated that he was going to kill himself. I got shivers down my spine, and the hair on the back of my neck stood up. I have heard these words from students before and always take them seriously, but my cop instincts kicked in immediately—this was more than just words. I asked him if he had a plan and what it was. He coldly stated how he was going to do it, and he had two contingency plans if the first one failed. We called the assistant principal into the situation and notified the father of the student. The student asked me to stay with him while we walked through the process with his dad. He was a single father who worked nights, so waking him up to come to the school was a little difficult, but he did manage to arrive. When the principal and counselor explained the situation, the father stated that his son was just acting out and wasn't going to do anything. He said that he was just seeking attention, and we were buying into it. I explained that I had had several interactions with his son, and it has never been like this before. I told him he was almost a different person than the student I was used to interacting with. Long story short, after several attempts, the father continued to deny that anything was wrong. Finally, he stood up, looked me in the eye, and said, "If you think it's a problem, then you take him." I was more than convinced that if I allowed the student to leave school that day, he would commit suicide. I took the student into PPC and took him to the hospital where he was screened into services. He stayed in the hospital while we had hearings as to where the courts thought he should go and who should have custody over him. He was eventually placed with his mother after he was released from the hospital. I spoke with him a few months ago, and he is doing awesome. He is married and has two beautiful kids of his own. He thanked me for everything I did for him that day and told me that not only did he have a plan, but he was also going to do it that evening. This was a success story for sure.

I have also found myself in very difficult situations where students tell a teacher that they don't want to go home for one reason or another. When I arrive, the teacher and principal already have their mind made up as to what I should do. I remember there were times where I would talk with a student, and while my heart poured out for them, there wasn't enough for me to actually remove them from the custody of their parents. It is a very difficult decision, and I still think about some of those situations and wonder if I made the right call. I would conduct safety checks in the home and talk with the parent(s) or guardian(s) to ensure that I did everything in possible to make sure the student was safe. Difficult conversations with educators would later arise about why I hadn't just removed the student. Again, I would tell them that, in my opinion, I just didn't have enough legal justification. I would refer them to CPS and tell them that I made a report as well. It was up to CPS to decide if they had enough to issue an ex parte to the court to ask to take custody of the child. I would also explain that it didn't mean I was done looking into the situation, and I would check in on the student and with the family to offer support wherever possible—It just meant I didn't have enough to remove the child at that time.

Those are the hard conversations to have. They are emotionally charged at both ends. For officers, it is important to understand that the work doesn't end by not removing the child in the moment. We can't just throw our hands up and walk away. We have to continue to work together, not only for that one student, but ALL students. Even when we do remove a student, the work doesn't stop. The child, as well as the guardians AND the current placement, all require help and resources. Working together as law enforcement and schools can better help everyone involved. My biggest advice in this section is to have a sit-down with all educators involved afterward. What was the goal in this situation? Why did officers take the child (or not take the child) into PPC? Moving forward, how can we work together to keep eyes on all students, and continually follow-up with students who are on our radar? There are things that both worlds can do. Again, it isn't about fighting the other person or being right, it is about getting on the same side and fighting the problem together.

The View from the Educator's World:

This topic is one of the hardest for me, and I still struggle with it today. It's also one that I have the hardest time leading staff through. In pursuing any level of degree, there are no classes that address the emotional toll that happens when a child shares the horrific stories that they are living every day or past traumatic they have endured. Some personnel who work in a school are more well-versed in these situations, such as counselors and social workers. However, in my experience, even they tend to struggle in these situations. Sometimes educators will notice a mark on a child and ask what happened. Most of the time, the response is something quite logical for children to get an injury from. Sometimes, a student will ask to speak with a trusted adult and will openly share things that are upsetting them. Other times, a student will blurt out something they believe is normal, but isn't, in the middle of a class discussion. At the older grade levels, a counselor or administrator will sometimes ask a student questions to try and solve attendance or grade problems, only to learn the real reason for the problem is related to something occurring outside of school. No matter how we get the information, educators are trained to be the mandated reporters, not the investigators. We take everything a child says at face value and make the report to Child Protective Services (CPS).

That should be simple, right? As educators, we hold no power to go to the home, take the child for medical evaluation, get involved in custody agreements, or remove the child from the current guardian's custody. If we weren't emotionally involved, it might be easy enough to make a report and trust that there is a system and process that will be followed by a state agency to investigate and determine the validity of the child's claims. The reality, however, is that sometimes the child tells you they are afraid to go home, or even worse, that they refuse to go home. For younger students, this often happens about 10 minutes before dismissal because that is about the time when they start thinking about leaving school for the day. Now, the student has really put the educator in a bind. The report can be made to the state agency, but very few are investigated the same day. This is where our emotions kick in, and we know that we must do more.

So, what is the next step? Calling for an officer. Now, this is where it gets sticky depending on the set-up you have with officers in your school and district. For districts who have their own Police Department or officers employed by the district, they typically have little jurisdiction over anything that does not occur on school property. Sometimes there is a Memorandum of Understanding between city or county departments that authorizes district officers to operate off school property when it pertains to a student in that district—but it can get pretty hairy for an officer to address something off property, not knowing what they are walking into. In my personal experience, I have worked for districts who have their own Police Departments. Those officers will go into the community when we are needing to locate a parent or student, but they will not go into a home to do an investigation pertaining to a situation that didn't happen on school property. This means we are now calling two different departments: our District Police Department AND the city or county Police Department. Based on my experience, the city or county officers do not like to conduct business in the school without a district officer on site as well, to make sure they are all on the same page. When we call for an officer from the district, their response time is typically under 20 minutes. However, as a non-emergent call for the city or county, sometimes this can be well over an hour.

Educators, pause and think about this: We must adjust our lens here. To us, this is an emergency. A student has reported abuse or neglect, and they are refusing to go home. While we believe the claims, they are making to be true because we know the student, and we KNOW that this student is not dramatic and would not lie—and maybe even the student has proof. However, pause and think about everything that is going on in the community that officers must also balance at the same time. It is very rare that your call will be deemed an emergency. I say this, to remind you that when the officers arrive on site, and they appear frustrated or annoyed as they walk in, it most likely has nothing to do with you or the situation. They might have just worked a call that involved someone dying, or maybe it was a high stress car chase. They might have been in their car for hours with no break. I will get into this more in the next chapter, but when officers arrive, I encourage you to first welcome them, thank them for coming, and ask if they need a bottle of water, soda, snack, chocolate, or to use the bathroom. We are all happier humans when our basic needs are met, and while it is not your job to meet their needs, they work in a car and don't always get to interact with pleasant people (More on this later though.)

Often, the next thing that happens in these situations is that the district officers and the city or county officers have a private meeting to discuss the situation. I will be honest—nothing makes me more infuriated than when they do this. By using other merges, I have learned that they are not intentionally doing this, but they are protecting the confidentiality of the situation. By this time, there are probably multiple staff members aware of the situation. If the student first reports to the classroom teacher, the classroom teacher then reports to either a counselor, social worker, or administrator. At this point, all parties are notified if the report is significant enough to warrant calling an officer. The administrator would then communicate to the other office staff regarding why police will be arriving. If there are any marks on the child or other bodily harm, the nurse is included as well. For educators, this team represents the typical crisis team that shares information to ensure continuity of care for all students. However, officers don't typically operate with a wide scope of others in a situation. When an officer arrives and moves into a separate area to talk to another officer, they are not doing this to have a secret conversation and exclude campus staff. When relating this to any other scene an officer responds to, the first officer on scene talks to the reporting party, and all other officers talk to that officer. It took me a long time to recognize this and to stop being offended by this act. If the student is in my office, then the officers must leave the room to have this conversation, which makes complete sense. Recognizing this protocol and helping other staff understand it has greatly improved our relationships with officers. Instead of entering situations on the defensive, we are more aware and appreciative of the methods they use to start the investigation.

Okay, so the officers have arrived and spoken to each other. Now it's time for the next sticky situation—meaning that the officers have to talk to the student. They prefer to do this in private. Again, this is not to exclude you. However, they have to hear the statement directly from the student without any coaching. Let's face it, as educators, it's our job to ask questions to students. Honestly, most of them are leading questions because usually we are coaching students with academic learning. In law enforcement, that is the worst thing that can be done. We don't recognize when we are doing it, and that makes having us in the room when a student is being questioned not an ideal situation. Another aspect to consider, is our relationship with the student—if the officer asks a question, and the student looks to us for reassurance, it may appear that the student has been coached on what to say. Why does this matter? Because if an officer places the student in Police Protective Custody (PPC), the student must again tell their story to a judge. If the officer cannot be on the stand and swear under oath that the student was not coached, then the testimony is not valid. As an educator, we mean no harm by this. Our intention is purely to make sure the student is safe. But as a parent, I would hope that an officer would not allow someone to coach my child and result in their removal from my care over something that was not true. While it doesn't make it any easier at the moment, I can logically work my way through this aspect when I remember that the officer must hear a statement directly from the student; they are the only ones who can ask questions.

Alright, so the officer(s) have talked to the student, and now they must decide. It's important to remember at this point (and this is where I struggle) that the decision is based solely on this report—it does not take into consideration past reports, situations, or the "teacher gut feeling" that we get as educators. While we are aware of other things the student has reported, or maybe other factors, that information is not considered in this report. Why? Because that is the job of CPS to investigate, if there has been a report made. If they weren't reported, then we can't say they should play a factor in the decision anyway. In all of my years as an educator, I have seen some horrible things happen to students, and I have very strong opinions about what could have or should have been done to prevent this. We all have seen situations in the news, and after they happen, a lot of people say, "we always knew ... but nobody did anything." My passion drives me in these situations, and it's when my emotional brain takes over. I have never had an officer put a student in PPC from the school. They have created safety plans with the family, done home checks in the evening with follow up at school the next day, and they have called CPS directly to try and move up the report. As an educator—when a student you know and love is looking at you scared to go home, feeling betrayed because they shared with you information that they hold most secret—you don't ever forget that look and feeling of pure helplessness.

> *As an educator—when a student you know and love is looking at you scared to go home, feeling betrayed because they shared with you information that they hold most secret—you don't ever forget that look and feeling of pure helplessness.*

Every time I am in this situation, I immediately begin to tell myself stories: "Clearly, the officers don't care about the student. They rushed the investigation. They didn't talk to the student long enough. They don't value my professional judgement." Not only do I tell myself stories, but I also allow staff to tell themselves these same stories and share them with other staff members. It's an emotional roller coaster and many of us lose sleep at night every single time.

But guess what? When I come home and talk to John,—, he always reminds me that the officers probably aren't sleeping any better for sending the student home either. The burden of proof must be so high that the officer would have to be certain that the student would die within 24 hours if they went home. That's a pretty big burden. It doesn't matter if we all agree with it or not, the bottom line is that if the PPC burden isn't met with facts that the student can share, then there is still time for CPS to investigate further and decide. John also reminds me of the statistics, and that when students are removed from the home on such short notice, it's often not a better experience for them. There are not a lot of emergency placements, and especially not ones that keep the student in the same school. If the student is placed in emergency placement, they now are removed from family, all of their belongings, and their school and friends. That's a lot for a student to process, and it's not the best option unless the officers are certain the student will die in a 24-hour window.

What I have had to learn, and am honestly still working on learning, is how to advocate for what we can do instead of focusing on the negative. First, when officers arrive, I ask them to please make sure one of them touches-base with me before they leave. This keeps me from hovering around trying to worm my way into the conversation. I back off, giving them their professional space, and take a breather to check on the staff who were involved. A few times, officers have had to leave in a rush for another call before they can connect with me, but they always leave their card so that I can call them.

Second, I always prepare myself for the possibility that the officers will not put the student in PPC. This allows me to get my emotions out of the way and return to my rational-thinking brain. While I will always make a call to them if a student says they don't want to go home, are scared to go home, or will run away if we send them home, I now work under the assumption that the student will, in fact, go home. This also helps me lead my team to start working on plans that support the student in the days ahead. We remain focused on what we can control instead of what we can't.

Third, when an officer tells me they are not placing the student in PPC, I do NOT ask why. Previously, this would always be my next logical question, but I've learned that since the officers arriving are ones who I rarely ever interact with, it may appear as if I am questioning their professional judgment. The fact is, it's really none of my business, and they don't have to justify their actions to me. Also, they really don't have the time to explain it in detail, so usually when I do ask that question, I get the response, "There is no imminent fear of death; the burden of proof could not be met." Which tells me nothing more than I already knew when they said they weren't going to put the student in PPC anyway.

Fourth, and most importantly, John has helped me with questions I can ask. Before working through this merge, any questions I would ask were questioning the judgment and decisions of the officer. Now, I ask questions that can help assure me there is a plan. In asking these questions, I have never encountered an officer without a plan, because again, they truly care about the student. I ask questions like:

- *Is there a safety plan in place?*
- *Have you made contact with the guardian?*
- *Can we schedule a welfare check for later tonight? (if needed)*
- *What is the follow-up plan?*
- *Can you contact CPS to fast track this report? (if needed)*

Fifth, I am always clear to thank the officers for their time. I also offer them another opportunity to use the bathroom, get some water or a snack, or even just sit down if they need to. If school is still in session, I will ask them if they want to walk around and spend time with students. Just like we sometimes hide out in classrooms or spaces with students who always make us smile, officers like to have positive interactions to offset the negative and hard ones. These small gestures show officers that we are on the same team, fighting for the same cause.

Am I perfect at this? John will tell you no, and that many times, I still call him in an emotional state because I'm just not able to process and understand why the burden of proof wasn't met. The caution here is that if I break relationships with officers who do not work for the district, those relationships are pretty impossible to fix. District employed officers are easy to get a hold of and typically work the same schedules and buildings even if they aren't assigned directly to a school. It's much more difficult to get in touch with city or county officers, and these interactions are typically less frequent. I know I have damaged some relationships because I've been using my emotional brain. Now I let this guide me in situations as much as possible to hopefully deter me from allowing my emotions to get the best of me while the officers are around. I'm a work in progress on this one, and probably always will be.

The Merge:

The merge here is stated simply, but it is difficult to accomplish. While we have different views on what a Child in Need of Care is, both sides want students to be in a safe environment. We have to fall back on this every single time. It looks different, and it might sound different, but if we stop fighting each other and work together to solve the problem, more will always be accomplished.

Because educators are often entering these situations with high emotions, this merge is only accomplished successfully if we have a strong relationship to fall back on. This is harder because it might not be the same officers who respond, but there are some protective measures listed above that will help safeguard the relationship. Nothing is ever accomplished because someone got emotional and started yelling, and nothing will drive an officer away quicker than educators acting irrationally. We must remember that we are coming from two different worlds. Educators are emotional when it comes to student safety. Officers are trained to not be emotional because emotions are not valid in court. An officer can't testify to a judge that the student was placed in PPC because the administrator used their "teacher gut feeling." The Officer might fully believe that more is going on than we know, but that is the role of CPS.

Educators, please remember that officers are on your side. Do not take their body language or curt conversations as anything other than that. This is just one of countless calls they will go on today. Advocate by asking questions, not passing judgement. Officers, remember that when educators are emotional, they really aren't mad at you. They are mad at the situation, and it is directed at you unjustly. Take the time to share what you can do to help in the situation to help the student. Remind educators that you don't like hearing or seeing these situations either, and what your burden of proof must be. Clear communication will. Help both worlds begin to merge in one of the most difficult situations there is.

> *Clear communication will help both worlds begin to merge in one of the most difficult situations there is.*

Discussion/Thinking Points:

- Educators: How do you recognize when you are in your emotional-thinking state versus your rational-thinking state?
- Educators: Have questions written down that you can ask Officers before they leave. This will help if you are still emotional.
- Educators: Remember that Officers who respond to your school are answering one of many, many calls in a day. Change your lens when looking at their interactions with you.
- Officers: Have you had a conversation with your administrators before an incident, or can you have one now to help explain your role?
- Officers: What other support can we offer in tense situations like these?
- Officers: How do we set aside our own feelings/beliefs when it comes to these situations?

CHAPTER 4

Building Relationships

This is arguably the most important chapter in this book; its only rival is chapter one. While building relationships comes almost as second nature to educators, it is much harder for officers. This partly why it is imperative to have the right person in the officer position. The SRO position is NOT a position to put someone in because of disciplinary action, a place to obtain a great work schedule, nor a position to "coast to retirement." The SRO position is probably one of the most important, if not the most important, position in the department. Even if you are not an SRO or an officer who responds to schools when called, think about this: You are tasked with making sure that a child's first interaction with law enforcement is a positive one! Being in a school-setting, law enforcement is tasked with basically living in the "5% other duties as assigned" category of the position description. Building relationships is one of the most important things law enforcement and educators can do to keep our schools safe. It is not just about building relationships with students but also about building and maintaining positive relationships between staff and officers.

Officers, please read this chapter with an open mind. We understand that everyone views working in schools in differently, but schools are a part of the community that you work in. If you are an officer who's placed full-time in schools, remember that any negative interaction you have will be unlike any you have experienced while working on the streets. On the street, if you arrest someone, you will most likely not see them all day, every day after that. However, that's not true for schools. If you have a negative interaction with a student, that student is still coming to school every single day. Think about that for a moment. Not only do we have to build positive relationships, but we also have to repair them when they are tarnished. I encourage you to be reflective on moments that could have gone differently if you had shifted your mindset or simply said yes in situations that would have cultivated positive relationships.

Educators, we are not off the hook in this merge at all. In all honesty, we are the gatekeepers of relationships that officers have with staff and students. Not only do we have to get out of the way, but we also have to open the door for this merge to happen. The way that you treat and talk about officers sets the standard for how your staff, and ultimately, the students will treat them. Having officers be a part of the positive climate and culture in your school will work wonders, and you will see the benefits of this relationship in a various ways.

While reading this chapter, please consider the different ideas that you can implement immediately to help foster a positive climate and culture in our schools. Everything else in this book, and in school, becomes so much easier when we understand that we are all on the same team trying to solve the same problem, supported by a solid relationship to fall back on.

The View from the Officer's World:

I will try not to make this chapter 87 pages because I know that if I included everything, I want to say about how important this topic is, it could easily become its own book! In my opinion, building and maintaining positive relationships with students is the number one thing we can do to keep our schools safe. It is the reason we are there! If a student heard something in the hallway, or saw something on social media, our hope is that they would tell an adult. We know that they won't just tell anyone, especially in this "I'm not a snitch culture." If that student had a strong, positive relationship with an adult that they felt comfortable approaching, the hope is that they would confide that adult, potentially preventing the incident from occurring. The phrase "See something, Say something" has been pushed out to schools for years now. We implore students to take action if they see something on social media, or if they hear something that is a threat to safety—we need them to say something. The trouble is, that theory only works if the students will actually share what they see with an adult who can help. Who better to approach with a safety concern than the law enforcement officer inside of the school? They are the one person whose job it is to make sure that we are safe! It seems simple, but again, without a positive relationship with the student, can we really believe that student will go to the officer in the moment of need?

> *Again, having a positive relationship with students so that they feel comfortable approaching an adult to share their problems or the problems of their peers, is the main objective.*

Again, having a positive relationship with students so that they feel comfortable approaching an adult to share their problems or the problems of their peers, is the main objective. Nobody can solve a problem that they don't know exists. The situation I hated most in school was when a parent would call me to tell me their child was having a problem at school. Whether that problem was harassment, bullying, or something else, it didn't matter; the parent was reaching to tell me something that was going on inside the school. Many times, I would get upset and ask the student why they didn't come talk to me at the time so I could help. Most of the time, I was met with the ever-popular "I don't know." It wasn't until I looked inward that I found the true problem lay with me. I should have been happy that the student had an adult in their life they trusted and could go to. I needed to change the way I did things to build stronger relationships with students so that instead of having to wait until they got home to discuss their problems, they felt comfortable talking to me. They were not the problem, *I was.* I needed to remember that they were CHILDREN, and I was the ADULT. It was my job to build the relationship and to never stop trying—even if there was a misstep along the way.

This realization caused me to change the way I approached my role. When I was an SRO, I had three rules for myself, and I still share them every chance I get to this day. If it wasn't illegal, no one would get hurt, and it didn't break policy, then my answer had to be YES. If you want to be pushed out of your comfort zone, I challenge you to follow the same rules as an officer. I promise that if you truly embrace it, you will see a change for the better in the climate and culture inside the schools where you work. This "rule" doesn't just apply to officers but educators as well.

Think about it in this type of context: I love chaperoning middle school dances. Everyone out on the dance floor is having a blast dancing to the upbeat music ... until a slow song comes on. Everyone leaves the dance floor except for the couples—and sometimes one of the girls' friends, who has to scream and take photos or videos to document the dance. As a former middle school boy, I always pay attention to the boys who would walk around the outside of the dance floor. I knew what they were doing because it's exactly what I did in middle school. They were trying to build up the confidence to ask a girl to dance. Eventually, the boy would make his way to the girl to ask that all-important question, and one of three different things would then happen:

1. A friend of the girl would see this happening from a mile away and grab her friend and run away.

2. The boy would ask the girl, she would say yes, and the middle school boy in me would cheer!

3. The girl would say no, and the boy would walk off defeated.

For this example, let's say the girl chooses option 3 and says, "no." My question is this: Is that boy ever going to ask that girl to dance again? Probably not. This seems like a weird analogy. However, keeping this in mind, if the dance team came up to me as an officer and asked me to dance with them in a basketball halftime routine, is it ok for me to say no? What if the drama club asked me to act in the school play, where they created a role just for me—" Officer John?" Can I say no? If I told them no to these simple things, how do I expect them to come to me when they hear or see something about school violence? Will they ever come to me to report? Or am I just another adult in their life that says I care about them, but won't really go out of the way to show them?

It is hard enough for officers to break down barriers without being viewed as the "hired-gun" on site. We need to do everything we can to be viewed by students and educators as another member of the team. I am blessed to be married to an administrator who understood this and supported the crazy things I got pulled into. One night during dinner, I got a phone call from the middle school band director at 6:00 p.m. The director and I had a decent professional relationship inside the school, and he knew I was a band nerd in my younger years and the instruments I could play. When I answered the call, he told me that the only tuba player in the middle school band was sick, and they had a concert in an hour. He knew I played the tuba and wanted to know if I could fill in and sight-read the music. I looked at Heather with a look that said, "It's dinnertime; I don't have to do this." However, because she understood the relationships I was trying to build in the schools and the larger community, she told me I had to go to the concert and play. So, I got up from the table, changed into my uniform, and drove to the school to play in a band concert. I did my best, and I enjoyed interacting with the students and community in a new way. The funny thing was, it didn't matter that I messed up the music; the out-pouring of support from the students and the community was unmatched. Parents came up to me with their kids after the concert and laughing and saying things like "We didn't know you could play tuba!" I got high-fives from the band students and their siblings. There were also social media posts made, allowing the whole community to see that I was invested in the lives of their children. To me, it is crazy to think about the impact that one quick, last-minute concert had because I honestly thought I was just helping the band director. It is amazing how one little act can mean so much to so many people. I often wonder what would have happened if I hadn't had a professional relationship with the band director, or if I hadn't said yes that night.

The impact didn't end there. About three weeks after the band concert, the middle school principal called me to the school. He made up some story about a goofy game at the all-school assembly that I "had to see." When I showed up to the school, he ushered me into his office. That should have been red flag number one, but at the moment, it didn't seem totally out of the ordinary. We talked about sports, family, and school stuff until he said, "Well, let's go watch this game." When I entered the gym, the Student Council representative began to talk. To be completely honest, I wasn't paying too much attention. I was just trying to figure out what kind of game they were going to trick me into playing, and I hoped it didn't end with a pie in my face. At one point, the student said, "Officer John," which brought my focus back. She began to talk about me, my position, and how much I meant to the school. I was confused, to say the least. I was there for a goofy game, yet they were only talking about me. Then the truth came out: the students and staff had voted me "Staff Member of the Month." The students cheered as They ushered me into the middle of the gym, and I was given a plethora of gifts. Those didn't matter to me (although the free Kansas City Royals tickets were awesome). I waved and smiled and tried really hard not to cry because I'm an emotional person. It meant so much to me that the staff thought of me as part of their family, and the students thought of me as part of their school. I was employed by the Sheriff's Office, not the school. Yet, here I was, being recognized as part of the staff.

Playing in the band concert continued to open more doors for me to participate in student and school events The request that pushed me out of my comfort zone the most was when a high school student came up to me and showed me a rap video about school zone safety. I remember his words as I gave him a confused look. He said, "Officer John, we can do better than this!" In my head, that CLEARLY broke the rule of being against department policy... Right? I called the Undersheriff right there and said, "I'm sure that me making a school zone rap video would violate policy, right?!" I mean, I gave him the answer! His response was indicative of the type of Sheriff's Office I worked for. He said, "Oh no it doesn't, but I have to be the first person to see the final product!" Well, my hands were tied at this point because the student heard I was given permission. We went and talked to the Audio-Visual teacher, who is a much better human than I am—When the student asked about creating a rap video, the teacher's eyes got big, and she immediately said "yes!" She turned the request into a semester-long class project. Students learned how to make digital music and sent me the track I was supposed to rap on top of. I took some time and wrote the lyrics. Yes, you read that correctly, I wrote the lyrics. When I was done writing and practicing, we recorded the rap audio track in one take. The students then brainstormed and created storyboards for how they wanted the video to look. We filmed the video, edited it, and with that, our first ever rap video was created. Again, it was amazing to see the final product and the impact it had on the climate and culture in the school building. A small school in Kansas, with less than 900 students in the entire district, created a rap video that now has over 4,000 views on YouTube. As you would expect, I got calls from the news media asking for interviews about the video. I was thrilled to share stories about the amazing things our kids can do. To be honest, it was nice to have a good news story to share, and the kids took so much pride in their work. They deserved all of the positive feedback they received in the process. The following year, it was no surprise, that students wanted to create another rap video. So, here I am now, 40 years old, and I am telling you, "Hello, my name is John Calvert, and I have two rap videos." But it is not about me. You see, both of these videos were created by students, and I could not be prouder of their efforts and the message of the School Zone Safety and Absenteeism Rap. Sure, the videos are funny. I mean, there's a cop, in uniform, talking about school zone safety and why it's important to not be absent from school. However, it got the community to listen to the same message in a different way. It was just one way that I could show the students, staff, and community that I was one of them. We were not fighting each other, but on the same side fighting the problems of students' low attendance and unsafe school zones.

Again, showing students, staff, and community members that you are on their side—that you are a part of the school family, and you want to build those relationships—is key to being a successful part of the school. We are not there to enhance any "school to prison pipeline," but to prevent the need for a situation to get that far. I tell anyone who questions putting officers in schools that I solved far more cases being in the schools than I ever did on the streets. Because I had built positive relationships with students, staff, and community members, everyone felt more comfortable coming to tell me things; they knew I was there for the right reasons. However, this meant I had a new level of responsibility. It was important that through investigations, I didn't accidentally destroy a relationship. This meant that when a student came up to me and gave me information, I respected their anonymity. Students would come talk to me and most of the time say, "You can't tell anyone I told you this." I had to pause and remember what it was like to be in school and how real the fear of retaliation was. I knew that I had to honor their wishes in every way possible. Students trusted me not to let others know they were the ones who "snitched." That is a lot of trust, and it would only take one mistake to ruin it with all students in the school. This was tricky, but I found ways around it. For example, if I used their information to try and get a search warrant and the judge wanted to know who gave me the information, I referred to the student as a "confidential informant." I would tell the judge that it was a juvenile who wanted to remain anonymous. If that meant I didn't get the search warrant, then so be it. I would need to find a different way to get more information. The most important thing was ensuring that I didn't violate the trust the students had in me.

Another thing to consider is the harm that is done when a relationship is damaged during an incident. In the moment, there might not be anything that we can do differently. However, if that happens, it is up to us, as officers, to repair it. Students are kids, and they are supposed to make mistakes. We are the adults; we are the ones who are supposed to be mature and model how to work through tough situations. It is important to not take things personally and to always show students that we are still on their side even when they mess up. Let's be honest, knowing that kids are going to make mistakes, we should want those mistakes to be when the consequences are less severe. Adult consequences are much different and often much more severe. As officers, it is part of our job to show students that we care about them and still want what is in their best interest—through the good times and the bad.

I think we have adequately addressed ways to build positive relationships with students, but they represent just one aspect in schools. Officers, whether you are stationed in one building or respond when called, you must remember to focus on building relationships with educators. This is not always the easiest thing to accomplish, and part of that is not our fault. Like any adult we interact with, many educators have personal biases about officers. These could be based on previous interactions, experiences, or things they have read or seen in the media. Regardless, when we walk into a school, we must be aware that not everyone might welcome us in. Over time, this can be changed just like any other relationship can. Let's dive deeper into how officers can build positive relationships with educators.

One afternoon, I walked into a classroom to drop off something to the teacher, not knowing there was a substitute that day. Either way, I needed to leave something for the teacher, so I made my way to the desk. The substitute was teaching a lesson on illegal searches and the protections offered by the 4th Amendment when one student asked a question. The substitute said, "Honestly guys, I don't know about that specific question." My ears perked up, and my eyes got big. I asked the substitute if I could answer the question for the student. I mean, as an officer, I live in the 4th Amendment. What should have taken me three minutes to explain, turned into a 20-minute question-and-answer session that lasted until the end the class. The bell rang for dismissal, and it brought me back to the realization that I had accidentally hijacked the class from the substitute. I apologized, and she told me it was not a problem; she wished I could have been there in previous classes to help answer students' questions. Even though she swore I had helped, I still felt bad. When I went back to talk (and apologize) to the teacher the next day, he told me the notes the substitute left reported how much she appreciated me taking time to talk to the class. That teacher invited me to talk to students about the Bill of Rights almost every year after that. He also happened to be in charge of the districts' Driver's Education program, and one day, he asked me to spend an hour talking about laws and traffic stops. After a quick conversation, that request turned into a four-hour block of a student presentation about traffic laws and traffic stops that included a time for mock car stops where students got to be "pulled over." We were able to go through what a traffic stop really looked like and answer questions in the moment. I explained what the officer was doing during each part of the stop, what we would like for them to do during each part of the stop, and more importantly—why! Through all of this, it was fantastic to be able to interact with students in a different way while creating a better relationship with this teacher. This experience also benefited me in the real world, as more deputies and officers shared that students were acting better when they would pull them over on the street. Slowly, because educators talk to each other all the time, this opportunity expanded into other opportunities in other classes. Sometimes this was purely fun, like being asked to be the 'guest donut taster' in Family and Consumer Science class. But other times, it involved serious topics like presenting to health classes the effects different drugs have on the body. The key takeaway is that these relationships grew in authentic ways over time, but it all starts with being a friendly face in the hallways as often as possible.

I will end this section by telling you a secret: In schools, educators find a way to make every single day a "food day." I remember arriving at a school one day, and the staff had a pot luck. I didn't know anything about it, and the administrative assistant told me that she wished she would have remembered to invite me to bring something. However, she always remembered after that. Now, I have always been one to play into the stereotypes about officers. So, any time there was a food day, no matter the theme, I always brought donuts. Italian potluck?

Here's some donuts! Mexican buffet? Donuts! No one ever questioned who brought them, and they were always eaten. This became a funny way for me to interact and be included in staff events, which in turn, made me a member of the school family. And honestly, I am a horrible cook, so it was a way for me to participate without having to put forth a lot of effort or worry about leftovers!

I've shared a lot about what officers can do, but the truth is, we need a lot of help from the educators to make this merge happen. My ask for educators is this: invite officers into classrooms to teach about different things. Who better to talk about searches and seizures or the First Amendment than an officer? Who better to speak about what to do during car stops in Drivers Education than an officer? Doing these things this helps students and the community view us as more than just officers—it shows that we are humans who care about students. Administrators, if we come to you with wacky ideas, please don't dismiss us. Building relationships looks differently for officers, and we need all the help and support we can get.

Officers, keep striving to find different ways to build relationships with students, staff, and the community. If it doesn't violate the three "rules," then I encourage you to say, "YES." It will be uncomfortable, and it will be nerve racking. Maybe it's not what we thought we would ever do when we got into law enforcement—However, breaking down barriers and showing our human side is another way we can keep our schools safe.

> *Building relationships should be (and probably is) at the forefront of every educator's mind at all times and in every interaction we have. Schools are the prime arena to build relationships with students and all stakeholders every single minute of every single day.*

The View from the Educator's World:

Building relationships should be (and probably is) at the forefront of every educator's mind at all times and in every interaction we have. Schools are the prime arena to build relationships with students and all stakeholders every single minute of every single day. If an educator chooses to not build relationships with students and colleagues, that is a choice (one that their administrators will address, I'm sure). Educators should have this one in the bag! The question we must ask ourselves is, "Do we afford officers who support our building that same advantage?"

Being married to a former school resource officer, I have always been aware of this. I made sure officers knew when we had potlucks, chili cook-offs, or when a community partner was providing lunch for the staff. And you know what? The officers always try to attend and are SO thankful to have been included. I have even had officers call and email me if they couldn't come, just so I knew they appreciated the invitation. At one building, these little steps made our school resource officer—who was assigned to support every school in the district—stop by our building almost daily. He knew teachers' and students' names and wanted to check in. He went above and beyond and was so visible that our teachers nominated and selected him to be our staff member of the month. The day he got the award will always be one of my favorite memories. We always presented the Staff Member of the Month award during our monthly whole-school assembly, and it was always a surprise to everyone (except administration) who won. His department wanted it to be a surprise for him too, so we strategically placed a "call for support" to get him to attend. I lost count of how many other officers arrived to help celebrate and congratulate him, and when he walked in the gym, we announced he was staff member of the month, he cried. It was just a piece of paper, and I honestly don't even think we laminated it, but it meant the world to him that our school appreciated him. At that moment, I realized that we, as educators, can't assume officers don't want to be a part of our staff. We just have to give them the opportunity to be, just like everyone we hire.

I love telling that story, and up to this point, educators are thinking, "Man... I could do that too in my building!" And you are correct. Simple items like that are easy. Add the officers to your staff email group (or the Sgt if you have many responding officers), and you can check that off the list, right? Throw in some personal invitations to new officers so they know you really mean it, and BAM—educators—we are off the hook!

Wrong. That's where I thought it stopped, too. Then one day the following situation happened, and I realized how much more work I had to do on this merge than others, and it still is something I struggle with. Here's what happened:

A first-grade student was out of control. Actively harming staff (punching, kicking, biting, throwing items at) on purpose. Destroying a classroom. An officer was called and responded. The officer stood and watched as I and others struggled to keep everyone safe and de-escalate the student. Was I upset that the officer didn't intervene? Upset doesn't describe it, I was irate. Could injuries have been prevented? Quite possibly. Did the officer do ANYTHING? Nope. He stood in the doorway and watched as staff took punches and kicks, resulting in staff injuries.

I want to pause the story here for a few clarifications before moving forward. Please know that I am not sharing this story to bash officers. First, each department will have their own guidelines on when officers can interact and restrain. It also can depend on the level of training an officer has completed at the time of the situation. Unfortunately, I was so angry I didn't ask these clarifying questions at the moment, and to this day I do not know why the officer did not intervene. However, looking back with a calm mind, I do not believe that it was the officer's intent for us to be injured while he just watched. Second, for those who might think, "Well, it was a first grader so how hard was the student actually hitting/kicking?" Hard enough to break one staff member's wrist and cause a hematoma so large in my leg that I was on crutches and in a walking boot for months.

Back to the story. This aggressive, out-of-control behavior went on for close to 45 minutes before the student's guardian arrived and took the student to a local crisis center. One staff member was sent immediately to the hospital for her wrist while the other staff helped clean up the classroom so that the class could return. I honestly could not tell you at what point the officer left, but it was probably when the student left. And that was probably best in that situation because nobody was ready to talk. (This is why having set weekly meetings is handy.) Once the room was cleaned, I began filling out injury reports. As I was doing this in my office, icing my own injuries, multiple staff members stopped by to ask what happened, check on the injured staff, see what duties needed covered, and offer any other support needed. Some staff who had walked by during the event stopped by to ask why the officer had just stood there and didn't help. Was I kind when speaking of the situation and the officer when other staff asked what happened? Not in the slightest.

And I was WRONG. To this day, this situation haunts me. Unintentionally, at that moment I ruined relationships between staff and the officer with my negative talk. What's more, for staff who do not get to interact with officers often, I ruined their view of the entire department. Just like we associate bad service at a restaurant with how the restaurant runs, we associate all officers with the actions of one. I was not a good leader at that moment, and I did more harm than I probably even recognize now. Officers should be treated like any other staff member. Would I have talked negatively about a teacher who did something I didn't agree with? Absolutely not. So why was it so easy to speak negatively about the officer? Because I still didn't view them as part of our staff. They were outsiders.

Here's a gut punch—do you negatively talk about the officers who support your building? If you have more than one, or a rotation, do you bother to ask their name when they arrive? Does your staff know when officers who support your building are helpful? Don't lie. Let's be real here because this is where I was failing. It's easy to send an invitation or engage with the items shared above. Those are a great first step, but we can't stop there. This merge was placed in chapter four intentionally. This must be said and worked on after you've read the first three chapters and worked through understanding how miscommunication and conflicting policies can harm relationships.

My hope is that you learn from my mistakes. I'll be brutally honest—I still do not agree with everything that officers do when they are responding to calls at our school. I don't know that I ever will, and that's okay. What I have been more aware of is controlling my emotions when I don't agree. First, I try to remember to ask questions before the officer leaves so that I have factual information (why did you not intervene?). If I don't have a chance to do that, then when staff ask me, I have a one-liner that I always use: "I don't know, there must have been a factor that led them to believe that was the best action at the time." Does this mean I don't call John or come home and give him an earful? Of course not! Sometimes he can help me understand, and sometimes he can't. At the end of the day, that's not the point or what matters most because it's not my job to understand all of the policies an officer must abide by. **What matters is that I give the same respect to our officers that I would give to any of my staff members, and that includes giving them respect, grace, understanding, and trust.**

The Merge

As an educator, we have to understand and respect the fact that officers don't really fit into the mold of school. Even if they are hired by the school district, they typically report to someone at an off-site location. School administrators don't often hire officers, nor do they train them or have time to include them in team building and the staff community. If we want officers to be involved and treat us like colleagues, it is a two-way street.

For this merge, the burden is on educators to take the first step. The bottom line: Officers can't build relationships when they don't have an invitation to do so.

- *Are officers who support your school included on your staff email group?*
- *Do you invite officers to staff and student celebrations at the school?*
- *Do you invite officers to staff happy hours, holiday parties, or other off-site celebrations?*
- *For officers that have more than one building: Does the officer know they can stop by to use the bathroom or get a bottle of water?*

• *Have you extended an open invitation for officers to pop in on classrooms? Or student lunches? Or be a part of student reward assemblies?*

• *Do you let staff know how an officer supported the school after situations? We don't need to share specifics, but a simple statement of "Officer Calvert responded to assist and support school staff" goes a long way.*

As officers, we must live by the three rules: if it isn't illegal, no one will get hurt, and it doesn't violate policy, our answer must be YES. Get into classrooms and interact with kids whenever and wherever you can. Participate in spirit week-themed days whenever you can. If a student or staff member builds up enough "guts" to ask you if you could do something, don't ruin a relationship by tossing it aside. Say YES! Building and maintaining positive relationships with our students and staff is the most important thing we can do to keep our schools safe.

Discussion / Thinking Prompts:

• Educators: What are special events that we can invite officers to? (hint....send invitations to them right now....)

• Educators: What is your view of officers who respond to support you? Does this match your view of other staff?

• Educators: In what ways can you make sure you are not damaging the relationship staff have with officers?

• Officers: How can we find ways to say 'yes' to more?

• Officers: What would it take for you to view yourself as part of the school family?

• Officers: How can you repair broken relationships with students or staff?

CHAPTER 5

Who's in Charge?

This question seems simple enough, right? We thought so too, but when we really started digging into why the officer and educator relationships were such a struggle, this topic was a point we just kept coming back to.

In a school, who is in charge? The administrator or administration team. Depending on the size of the school and the district, this could be a principal, assistant principal, or even superintendent. However, any educator will openly tell you that a decision is rarely made in a school without the administrator first consulting with other staff. If it's a decision about curriculum implementation or instructional practices, the administrator will consult with the instructional coach, building leadership team, or teacher teams. If it's a decision relating to student behavior, the administrator will typically consult with the counselor, social worker, building leadership team, or teacher teams. The point is that in any school, administrators rarely make a decision without consulting with someone else. However, at the end of the day, decisions fall to the administrator to make the final call and to defend that decision if necessary.

When an officer shows up to a scene, whether it be on the side of the road or at a residence, we immediately assume full control over that situation. It helps keep us and everyone else safe, and it is what we are trained to do: Take control and ensure safety. We show up; we separate individuals; we gather statements, and nothing happens unless we have given permission. While we have discretion to use our judgment, officers typically have our own guidelines for how we will respond in situations. Rarely do we call for a supervisor to double check what we are doing, and we are not used to having our decisions questioned or second-guessed. This becomes very uneasy when we show up in a school and are asked to justify the decisions we are making.

As we worked through our situations in real time around our dinner table, we realized that the struggle we both had to merge our worlds came as we both felt we should be in charge of the situations. Moreover, as an administrator and officer, we were both trained and expected to be in charge by our superiors. If you've read this book in order, you have encountered moments where we say the worlds might remain separate—such as in Chapter 2, where we discussed what happens when a student breaks a law on school property. You've also read about moments when we urge the worlds to work side-by-side, such as in Chapters 3 and 4, where we discuss navigating children in need of care calls and building stronger relationships. In the end, this work is messy because determining who is in charge will change based on each unique situation. That is clear as mud, but we will tear this down further throughout this chapter.

The View from the Officer's World:

I remember being in field training as a brand-new officer. I would openly share my thought process so my training officer could hear what I was thinking or what I was going to do and provide feedback. We would respond to calls and after we would get all the facts, I could go back to my training officer and talk it out. After hearing everything, sometimes the training officer would share his opinion; sometimes, he would just nod in approval and say something along the lines of, "Get it done." I remember laughing the night I entered my last phase of training. I went to the very first call of the night, gathered all of my information, knew what I was going to do, and went back to discuss with my training officer. I told him all the information I had gathered and what I was about to do when he said, "Hey Calvert, I'm not here. Do whatever you think you should do, just don't get us killed." It was a completely different feeling, but he was exactly right. When I completed my training, I was going out on shift in a car by myself, and sometimes, I would be the only one out for the entire department. I would not call my supervisor every time I stopped a car. I was in charge; I owned the car-stop, and I owned the situation. It was mine. I used my voice to take control and command the scene when I showed up. My decisions were final.

It's not surprising that, like many officers, I had this mentality when I showed up in school for the very first time. I quickly realized that a school is a much different place than the streets. The hierarchy was not spelled out like I was accustomed to. Again, I was hired by a Police Department, not the school, so my supervisor rarely came to the school. The Superintendent, however, was partially responsible for my evaluations. I remember this internal struggle of questioning what my chain of command was. What can I tell the teachers, counselors, assistant principals, principals, superintendent, and when? They can't tell me what to do, and I don't need them to make decisions for me, but how do we work together?

This is when I had to shift my mindset. We needed to work together to keep our schools safe. School safety isn't a one-person job, it is everyone's job. When I showed up at the schools, it wasn't like I was asking permission to do things (and the educators didn't make me feel I needed to). However, when we started building relationships with each other, it became second nature to fill-in the administration what I was going to do that day or if I was handling a situation. Just the same, if there was something the administration was hearing or concerned with, they would give me a heads up. This became an act of mutual respect between us, and neither side viewed it as asking for permission.

This was put to the test whenever an administrator called 911 or asked for the officer directly. As officers, it is very easy for us to show up to the office, classroom, or hallway and snap back into the mentality that we are responding to a call and are in charge. Once I show up, I am trained to take control. Some situations inside of a school call for that if safety is a concern. We get called to an unruly parent or a fight in the bathroom, and when we show up, we may have to take control and own the situation until things calm down. These are highly stressful situations and officers are trained to handle them appropriately. It is important to remember that even though we feel like we should own a situation, we are literally in someone else's world who has been entrusted to own that situation as well.

Instead of fighting about who is in charge and when, I urge you to change your mindset. About five years into my time as an SRO, I showed up to the middle school for yearbook picture day. I always had fun with these photographs because my mom didn't care about them anymore, so there was nobody to yell at me if the picture was bad. It was even better because the school didn't hire a photographer, but instead, had a staff member take them. This meant that she already knew everyone who needed a picture taken. After I finished taking my funny photograph, the principal, counselor and I took some funny "family photos." It wasn't until a few weeks later when I received a poster of one of the photos where the principal was sitting in a chair, the counselor was standing behind her, and I was standing in the back. The caption at the bottom read, "One Team Linked for Success." I laughed at first glance, but when I had a moment to step back and think, it was really amazing. Staff members didn't see us as an administrative team and officer, but as one team. We were all there for the same reason: the safety and well-being of our students and staff members. This poster was one way I knew I was breaking down barriers and walls within the building.

Unfortunately, there are some aspects in our profession where we can't share exactly what is going on. Sometimes, information shared could be a violation of privacy, an ongoing investigation, or break a juvenile code. In these moments, we have inadvertently put up barriers that impact the safety of our students or staff because we can't share exactly what is going on. While I didn't know what *"Handle with Care"* was at that time, I am a huge proponent of letting the appropriate people know if one of our students or staff may be going through a tough time. For example, I would get emails from other deputies or officers who worked a call where a school-aged student was present. Some would include the entire narrative; other emails would just include the pertinent facts. So, when I arrived at school, I would read an email where a deputy responded to a domestic violence call in progress, and they arrested both parents who were involved. The call initiated at 11:00 p.m., parents were arrested at 11:20 p.m., and the kids were placed with auntie, uncle, child protective services (or whomever) at 3:00 a.m. This would be great information for educators to know, because if the students came to school that day, it was going to be a tough day. I would simply walk to the principal and counselor and say, "Johnny might have a rough day today." That way if Johnny came to school and acted out, or fell asleep in class, or whatever else may have happened, the educators who needed to know understood that there was something else going on behind the scenes. Instead of assigning consequences, this allowed everyone to show Johnny some grace and kindness. Maybe he needed to go to the nurse's office and take a nap. Maybe he needed breakfast or a snack. The same went for the educators. If the counselor came to me and said that a student might have a tough couple of days, I didn't need to know all the ins and outs of everything. I trusted the counselor and knew that if she thought I needed to know something specific, she would tell me. Establishing this quick and easy communication between myself and the educators ensures that we are on the same team.

Around my third year in the SRO role, my wife asked me to attend a conference with her. This was a conference for educators, but they had sessions on student absenteeism, so the department agreed to send me as well. I have to be honest—I didn't think I would get anything from this conference, but Heather was sure I would love it. As usual, she was right. One important thing to remember is that every repeated behavior receives some form of reward, which is often true upon reflection. When I step back and really think about this, it is totally accurate. Educators have this figured out, but it was new to me. I began looking for examples of this in schools and found so many. Educators are really good at rewarding student behavior. Students get individual rewards and classes earn parties or free time. While this is common at the elementary level, middle and high school students also receive rewards for having no tardies, no missing assignments, and good grades in each class. Educators strive to reward positive behavior so that students will repeat it. On the flip side, we are also great at rewarding bad behavior. It's not uncommon for students to be sent out of class or to the principal's office when they disrupt the class. One time, I realized I was responding to calls frequently for the same student. I started forming a positive relationship with him very early in his educational career, but one year he was especially volatile. Almost daily, it seemed, he would try and throw chairs or other items across the room. He would often hide under tables as staff would try to direct him to another room. I would show up and talk with him, and in a matter of seconds, I would get him where he needed to go and defuse the situation. Again, this is part of that "5% other duties as assigned." I wasn't going to arrest the student or write a report, I was simply there to offer support and assist the educators. And, if I do say so myself, I was doing a fantastic job! After one instance, I was patting myself on the back as we exited the classroom, and the principal looked at me and said, "John, I need you to not respond anymore." WHAT?! I was the one the student listened to! I was the one the student would calm down for, and you want to remove me from helping? I think I communicated this to the principal by saying, "Uhhhh, what?!"

This was when I recognized the importance of this merge. Because the principal and I had a great relationship and had worked together for a few years, he felt very confident in telling me that I was actually the problem and not the solution—I needed to let the staff be in charge. The student wasn't calming down because I was there, he was acting up because he knew that I would respond. That was his reward, he got to hang out with me for a few minutes. I went from thinking I was in control and helping, to realizing that I was the one causing the issue. The merge here was simple. I wouldn't respond to the situation unless I was specifically called. We made a deal with the student—if he went a certain number of days without an incident, then I would come hang out with him on the playground, eat lunch with him, or give him a five-minute break from class to walk the halls and hang out.

Both sides need to remember that there will be times that we work together and are both in charge, but there will also be times that we have to let the other party be in charge.

When I was an SRO, I was lucky enough to be assigned to the entire county. I was in charge of three different districts totaling eight school buildings. There were times where other deputies or officers had to respond because they were closer, but I was the one who would take over when I arrived. I was lucky enough to be able to build relationships with the educators in each of these schools, so that when we had to determine who would be in charge of each situation, we could do so without damaging relationships. Heather has it a little harder because she gets a different officer on nearly every call she makes. For officers, it is important to understand that no matter what our situation is, our stance should be the same. We are here to fight the problem, NOT each other. It doesn't matter our position or title; we must work together and show everyone that we are a team ready to offer support. Is this a difficult merge sometimes? Yes! Did I make mistakes as an SRO that I could learn from and do better the next time? Absolutely! We get to work together. We get to keep everyone safe. **We get to be a team.**

The View from the Educator's World:

One of the first things my mentor told me as I moved into the world of school administration was it can be a very lonely job. At the time, it sounded so odd to me, because even if I was the only administrator on site, I would have other administrators I could call from other buildings. After almost ten years in the administration world, I now believe the answer lies somewhere in the middle of those two views. For most school administrators, we move up the ladder from a classroom teacher position. There are many steps along the way that vary depending on your district and level, but include positions like instructional coach, intern, activities director, curriculum coordinator, assistant principal, associate principal, etc. Each of these positions is different depending on the size of the building and district, and every building administrator enters their first position drawing from a different background and experiences.

Taking the first administrator job is a shock similar to that of the first classroom teaching job. Even with all the course work and preparation, walking into my first classroom and knowing that there was no safety net of a cooperating teacher anymore was a scary feeling. Similarly, being hired as a building principal for the first time, knowing the responsibility that comes with that role, was also a scary feeling. I have learned in my time, just like many of you have, that the success of any school administrator is to build a team that can be trusted. This helps lighten the burden of all the impossible tasks that are on an administrator's to-do list. However, at the end of the day, if someone I have trusted to complete a task doesn't get it completed, it's still on me. Or, if someone else decides, the consequences of that decision will fall upon me as the building administrator. It's a very complex and stressful world to live in, and it gets messier when we invite officers into that space.

For officer's reading this, I want to pause here and share some information that you probably are not aware of. It doesn't matter if the officers are stationed at the building, if they work for a District Police Department, or if they work for the City or County Department. When an administrator decides to involve an officer in a situation, there has already been a lot of thought before making that call (unless it pertains to a weapon, or another significant crime has been committed). In our personal lives, most people rarely put much thought into calling for help from any emergency agency. However, as a school administrator, there are many consequences from involving those same agencies in a school with students. Some of these consequences are positive and some are negative.

Let's start with an easy scenario: medical emergencies. If anyone on school property is having a medical emergency, or is even in medical distress, I will always err on the side of caution and call 911. I always tell staff it's better to be safe than sorry, and I would rather have people on site who are much more knowledgeable than I am, just in case. We usually have the local fire department respond first, followed by EMS, and then officers. We also have the guardians for the student, or the emergency contact for the staff member, on the way as well. My role as the administrator is honestly more of the scene manager in these instances. Sometimes, we make the call to clear the halls to protect privacy as well as ensure those that are involved in the crisis can move easily if needed. In my years as an administrator, I have never had anyone get upset or file a complaint because I called for medical help, even if we don't end up needing someone to be transported to a hospital. In fact, a simple report is made to inform my superiors, and an even more simple communication blast is sent to all families that just states there was a medical emergency at the building and it caused a minor disruption to the school day. I never get questions, phone calls, or complaints.

This differs vastly from if community members, staff, or students see a police car parked outside that isn't normally there. Everyone wants to know why there is an officer on site. Did something happen? Is everyone safe? Was a student arrested? Personally, I believe this stems from what seems like constant news reports of violence in schools and communities. Our brains have been programmed to associate an officer's presence with a horrible event occurring. For some, this also could be based on lived experiences. I will admit that if I drove by my children's school and saw a police presence (even just one car), I would immediately wonder what happened. I don't give any thought to the idea that maybe, it's an officer who just stopped by to build relationships. Even at the high school that has officers assigned to it full time, my first thought is always that something must have happened. Even when I see an officer's car at a local restaurant, I don't assume they are just getting lunch for themselves. Nope, I assume that something has happened inside, and it's probably not safe at the moment. When you stop and think about the stories we tell ourselves as a society, I don't know that we can change this, especially not with this book alone. Hopefully, the more that we invite officers into our schools, we can slowly change this perception. However, until that happens, administrators are faced with the reality that when we make a call to have an officer support a situation, there will be inquiries why we made that call.

Administrators know we will potentially get backlash from a variety of stakeholders, depending again on the community in which you work. I have been told by my superiors before to stop calling for officers to help support situations, and that I must have prior approval before calling. I have been on the receiving end of hysterical, irate parents and community members for having a police presence in the school. I have watched staff and student demeanor shift as an officer walks through the building. These are big walls, and again, they will not come down because we wrote this book. It doesn't mean that we need to stop trying, or that we allow our officers to take the brunt of all of the possible ramifications of calling them. I can promise, when you call them, they are arriving on scene to help.

Okay, so we made the call to get support from an officer, already having internally battled all the above. Now we wait for an officer to arrive. I have found there are two different viewpoints from this point forward. The first is where I reside, and typically, when I have asked for help, means I am exhausted and ready to hand the situation off to the officer. The other view is the administrator, who wants to tell the officer what to do and how to handle the situation, because they are entering "my school." Let me tell you, neither of these views is productive. When I think back to my first few years as an administrator, and the interactions I had with officers when they arrived to a call at my school, I have to laugh. I'm sure if you had recorded it, the situation would have appeared like an awkward first date. The officer arrives on scene, enters the office, and doesn't even know what to say other than "I'm responding to a call." Office staff connect the officer to me, and neither of us knows what to say. Why? I assume the officer can read my mind or intuitively understand the situation and know what I need. The officer is uncomfortable, doesn't understand why we didn't just call a guardian, and probably wants to leave as quickly as possible to get back to their comfort zone. This might still be the current situation for many of you, but don't worry, it will get better!

As we discussed in Chapter 4, when the officer arrives, provided the situation is safe and under control, offer them water and guide them to a space where you can update them on the situation. Administrators, at this point, we are still in charge. We must communicate the entire situation clearly, accurately, and as briefly as possible so that the officers can assess what is needed by them. I would advise you to keep this initial conversation between you and the officer, as other staff members just muddy the water. If the officer needs to talk to them, they will ask. Also, if the situation ever were to go to court, everyone who talks to the officer might have to testify. I always tell my staff that fact when they feel left out or excluded from the situation. It takes practice sharing just enough information so that the officer can make an informed decision, but not too much information that we end up wasting time. If you have an officer that responds frequently to your calls for support, I urge you to talk to them and work together on this to make sure that both sides feel comfortable giving feedback. If, like me, you don't have the same officer who responds frequently, then start the conversation by stating that you want to respect their time, but if they need more information, please ask.

Once the situation has been communicated, we have to give up some of the control. If you need something specific from the officer, such as contacting the guardian because you lack a working phone number, be sure to communicate that clearly. This instantly communicates to the officer that you aren't asking them to solve the problem with the student, you just need help locating a parent. They can get to work on that immediately. If you are needing help addressing a behavior, I have learned to ask questions rather than make general statements such as, "I need the student to stop running around the school." The officer doesn't possess a magic wand to make that happen and will likely just look at you in response. As discussed in previous chapters, this is where effective communication is key. We must work together to find a solution that makes sense.

The Merge

Here's the million-dollar secret: *To merge our worlds, we actually both need to be in charge at the same time.* Each of our worlds have different options available and we each have different skill sets. Because of that, we must draw upon each other's professional expertise to effectively keep our schools safe. If we spend time battling each other for who gets to be in charge, we both lose.

Having a relationship with the other position to ask questions or communicate needs is imperative to making this merge. Simply asking questions, such as, "Can we do this?" or "Here's what I'm thinking, what are your thoughts?" gives us the time and the space to work together to attack the situation. With everything that both sides are dealing with from day-to-day, it should be viewed as helpful that we get to work together. Administrators and officers should share a lot of the same knowledge of a situation, but working together helps fill in any gaps in understanding that one side may have.

> *Administrators and officers should share a lot of the same knowledge of a situation, but working together helps fill in any gaps in understanding that one side may have.*

Finally, recognize when the other needs to be completely in charge. For officers, if a law hasn't been broken, let the educators take control. For educators, understand that if safety is a concern, the officers will need to assume command. Knowing this ahead of time, and even talking out situations before they occur, will prevent these moments from damaging the relationships that have been built.

Discussion / Thinking Prompts:

- Educators: What personal experiences with officers are you bringing into your role? How do you manage any bias you may have?
- Educators: Practice giving clear and concise information regarding situations.
- Officers: How can we give up the "my scene" mentality?

• Officers: How can we take the time to explain why we did or did not do something without breaking confidentiality?

• Officers and Educators: How can we put roles aside and be viewed by all as a team and not individuals?

Time for Dessert

We purposefully did not name this section "Conclusion" because this work will never be done or completed. School safety is a journey, not a destination. It is not a place that we can ever arrive at, plant a flag, and say that we have conquered it. Keeping our schools' safe is ever changing, ever evolving, and involves us working together. Just because your title or position puts you in one world, does not mean that you have to alienate the other world. The most important thing we hope that you take away from this book is that we are not on this journey alone, and it won't be easy to merge the worlds. We have each made mistakes throughout our careers while trying to navigate this work. We learned from our mistakes, reflected, and we made adjustments. To be honest, we continue to make mistakes, but we have never stopped working together to ensure we are focused on merging our worlds. Both worlds bring such different and needed perspectives when it comes to safety in our schools, and that must be valued. Our hope is that while you read this book, you are able to take what we have said and mold it into something that can cause meaningful change in your respective positions.

> *There is not one school or district that looks the same as another. However, the love for education and the well-being of our students and staff is something we should use as leverage to merge our worlds together.*

There is not one school or district that looks the same as another. However, the love for education and the well-being of our students and staff is something we should use as leverage to merge our worlds together. It has been stated several times throughout this book, but we will say it again here: We are truly on the same team. So often, we feel we have to fight each other, or that the other side is the cause of the problems we have. In all honesty, the moment we can change that mindset and realize that we are on the same team, fighting the common problem, we will see great strides in the climate and culture in our schools.

Thirteen years later, and our dinner table is still the place where we continue to hash out our struggles. It's still the place where we have tough conversations. We continue to work together to solve the problems we encounter, even when it makes us really uncomfortable. Our kids have bought into this, and as they get older, the more of a voice they find in what is going on in their world as well. Our passion for this work developed because we couldn't quit when it got hard. We couldn't move schools, ignore each other, or just agree to disagree. No, we are married first, and our jobs are second. We are both deeply passionate about the work we do, and it is around our dinner table that we realized we could be doing so much more by working together.

We hope that this is only the tip of the iceberg for you. We hope that you take to heart what is written back to your world and continue to push this work forward because there is so much more to be done. For example, why do we still often separate officers and educators in training pertaining to school safety? Why can't an officer attend a school conference, or an administrator attend an SRO conference? The learning that can take place by spending time together learning about the other world can only help with merging them together.

As you finish reading this book, please reach out to the other world and schedule a meeting. If there has been confusion in the past, or situations that have hindered the relationship, take this time to clear the air. Use this meeting as a jumping point to refocus and create a plan on how we can best begin merging our worlds and working together. In today's world, school safety is too important to make excuses. *We thank you for all you do for our schools and communities, and we pray that you found this book helpful and begin to see a shift in how you work together. Thank you for spending some time at our dinner table. When you have scheduled your meeting, you are excused.*

Appendix/Scenarios

Our hope with this added section is that once you are done reading the book, you have some time to sit down with the other world and work through some very high-level scenarios. As we stated throughout the chapters, working through situations before they occur will ensure that all voices are heard and all perspectives considered. We encourage you to use what you have learned with the five merges to talk openly and honestly about what your world may need from the other world, and take the time to apply what you are hearing to possible scenarios that you may encounter in the future. Feel free to add in frequent situations that you encounter while you are working through these to make the scenarios real for you.

Scenario One:

It is the middle of lunch when two students stand up and start physically fighting. Before anyone has a chance to react, there is a large crowd that has formed around the fight. No trays or weapons are being used at this time, just fists.

1.*What are the first steps for you?*

2.*If an officer arrives first, when do you contact the administrator? Educators, if an officer is not on site, when (if at all) is the officer contacted?*

3. *Would it change anything depending on who the students were?*

4. *How would it change if the officer or administrator was present during the lunch hour?*

5. *In your opinion, what is the desired result?*

Scenario Two:

The school contacted the parents from the lunchroom fight above and asked them to come pick up their students. The parents arrive on campus at the same time and words are exchanged before they ever make it to the front door. One parent buzzes into the office and states, "I need to pick up my kid before I beat this guy up." This angers the other parent, and a physical fight ensues at your front door—luckily, before either parent was allowed into the building. No weapons are currently present.

1. What is the immediate school response?

2. If an officer is on site, what is their immediate response?

3. Who is intervening and when?

4. What are the responses from both the school and officer?

5. Is there a way to change our practice now to try and avoid this scenario?

Scenario Three:

With two minutes left before classes switch, there is a call of a Medical Emergency in the hallway by the gymnasium. A custodian calls out that a student fainted and is currently unresponsive.

1. Educators: In order, what steps do you take? What are others doing?

2. Officers: What do you do, and when?

3. What conversation should occur with all staff prior to an event like this?

4. Who on-site is CPR and/or AED trained?

5. Does the officer have immediate contact with responding medical services? Knowing the school best, what supports can you offer both worlds?

6. Who is staying with the student, and who is helping guide medical services into the parking lot and building?

Scenario Four:

There is a call over the radio of a disruptive student who is refusing to leave the classroom. The teacher states that the student continually used profane language during the lesson, and when asked to leave the classroom, he stated that he wasn't going anywhere. The classroom still has the rest of the class inside.

1. *Educators: At what point do you call for an officer?*
2. *What is the end goal of both worlds?*
3. *What are our options to get back to a normal day?*
4. *What support are you (in your role) needing from others?*

Meet the Authors

John Calvert is a husband of an educator and father of two. He has a Bachelor's Degree in Criminal Justice and was a full-time Law Enforcement Officer for 12 years. During

that time, he was a School Resource Officer for 6 years. John is currently the Director of School Safety for the Kansas State Department of Education and a part-time Law Enforcement Officer. John is a national speaker who focuses on empowering educators, law enforcement, and students to build positive relationships to keep our schools safe. He is recognized by the United States Department of Education's Safe and Secure Schools Unit as a Subject Matter Expert in School Safety.

Dr. Heather Calvert is a wife and mother of two. She graduated from Kansas State University in 2006 with a Bachelor's Degree in Elementary Education. She later earned her Master's Degree in Curriculum and Instruction, her Doctorate in Educational Leadership, and a Certificate of Equity. She has served as a classroom teacher, Instructional Literacy Coach, Building Leader Intern, Assistant Principal, Principal, and Principal Coach. She has also been an Adjunct Professor at Fort Hays State University. Heather has presented on a national level about a variety of topics dealing with education. She has also published numerous articles.

How to Connect with the Authors

Email and Social Media

info@calvertenterprises.com
Facebook: @CalvertEnterprises
Twitter: @heathercalvert @officerjohn326
@CalvertEnt1

Speaking Engagements and Pricing Information
Email: info@calvertenterprises.com or visit
https://www.calvertenterprises.com